Grant Writing
DeMYSTiFieD®

Mary Ann Payne

New York Chicago San Francisco Lisbon London Madrid Mexico City
New Delhi San Juan Seoul Singapore Sydney Toronto

About the Author

Mary Ann Payne is a true generalist who is adept at connecting community resources with small, nonprofit organizations in new and creative ways as she creates positions for herself to match her changing interests and family circumstances. During the last 20 years, she has focused on writing successful grant proposals for school district child development programs and small human service nonprofit agencies with awards ranging between $1,000 gifts from family foundations to multi-million dollar federal grants. She is particularly proud of her ability to train agency staff in grant writing so they no longer need her services and she can move on to new challenges. Although she has written many training manuals and conducted numerous workshops, *Grant Writing DeMystified* is her first book.

Ms. Payne's formal education includes a bachelor's degree in liberal arts from the University of Chicago, graduate work in human development from Pacific Oaks College, and intensive training conducted by the Grantsmanship Center in Los Angeles. She is an active volunteer with Upland-Foothill Kiwanis and a proud member of the Inland Empire Chapter of the Grant Professional Association. She and her husband live in Ontario, California.

Contents

Preface

Grant writing is like a cross between preparing a holiday dinner and running a marathon. The process takes stamina, perseverance, focus, and a lot of effort before the big day. In fact, it takes more preparation than you can ever imagine, especially if you've never done it before. There are coaches and recipes and strategies, however, and that's what this book is about. I've written dozens of successful grants over the last 20 years and my extremely high success rate shows I've learned a few tricks of the trade. Many of them have already been written down—and I'll direct you to those resources. Some of them are tips I've stumbled across from sources I've forgotten. Others are ideas I've collected from friends and colleagues and strangers who also write grants. I've organized all of these "recipes" in a chronological sequence much like you create a menu or training schedule. You'll need to do the actual work (defining your project, collecting information and documents to explain its value, finding funding sources, and finally creating a budget and writing the narrative), but I can be your trusted aunt who teaches you how to make a three-layer cake or hard-nosed coach who sets the training schedule day after day.

In the fairness of full disclosure, however, I can't promise the roast will be cooked to your guests' tastes or that you'll win the race. Most foundations receive 10 to 15 times as many requests for funds as they can meet. Government dollars are even more competitive in certain fields. There are dozens of factors that go into funding an application and many of them are out of your control. What I can do, however, is provide tools and strategies to ensure your proposal is noticed and taken seriously. If the potatoes are a bit dry, we'll add more milk next time. If you place fourth in your age category and they only award three medals, we'll tweak the training schedule before the next marathon.

If your proposal is not funded the first time, we'll review the rating comments, talk to the program officer, find a different foundation, tweak the words a bit, and try again.

This Book Is Not for Everyone

The Internet and bookstores are filled with materials to help grant writers at all stages of their professional development. What makes this book unique is its focus on the planning stages that are often assumed to be common knowledge. *Grant Writing DeMystified* will be of most value to:

- Executive directors, program coordinators, or board members of nonprofit 501(c)(3) organizations with responsibility for but little experience in writing grant proposals
- College seniors or graduate students seeking money for their first independent research or study project
- Principals and teachers in public and private K to12 school districts who want to replace programs eliminated by budget cuts or offer enrichment activities to their students

Grant Writing DeMystified will be of less value but still useful to:

- People now engaged in community service who have not formed a 501(c)(3) corporation but have at least three years of documented results
- Individual artists, writers, musicians, and others pursuing solitary pursuits
- Principal investigators who mentor beginning grant writers
- Coordinators of system-wide grants programs for community colleges and school districts who are looking for materials to explain the grant-writing process to faculty and staff
- Nonprofit consultants, workshop leaders, and short-course teachers who want a resource textbook to enhance their work with adult learners
- Business owners who are willing to partner with a research group or nonprofit agency to provide specialized training, employment, or product development services. (Loans are scarce and difficult to obtain and there is *no grant money* for entrepreneurs to start their own business.)

Personal Quirks You'll Find as You Read

Grant Writing DeMystified is written in a conversational style with lots of stories and the use of personal pronouns. I do this for a variety of reasons.

- **Stories** are easier for me to remember than facts. I also encourage you to collect your own stories. If a proposal is successful, a story or two will help you repeat the effort. If you had an unsuccessful experience, stories will help you remember what to do differently next time. The specific details in your stories will be different from those in mine but the concepts remain the same so I'll provide the concepts and leave the details to you.

- **Personal pronouns** help me remember that real people are reading this book. Hopefully it will also help you see me as a guide to understanding a path we're following together rather than as an "expert" with all the answers. Occasionally I'll slip into the royal "we." That's because I have a vested interest in your success in securing the financial support and other resources you and your organization need. I plan to be with you every step of the process to guide, cajole, and rekindle the passion when it wavers. Thank you for allowing me to join your quest.

- **Examples** will be numerous because I believe concrete representations are more effective than abstract ideas. Your responsibility will be to substitute your particular details for those I use.

- **Sample** documents and activities like brainstorming, setting up files, organization charts, and budget pages, will be almost simplistic. This is not to insult your intelligence, but because I find it easier to move from simple to complicated rather than vice versa. Government RFPs (requests for proposals) are notoriously more convoluted and difficult to decipher than foundation guidelines—and there are broad differences between government departments and among family foundations. I'll be using the simplest, most straightforward ones as samples so we can identify the common elements easily without getting lost in bureaucratic language and jargon.

- **No sample letters of intent (LOIs) or grant proposals** are included in the book, although I suggest you locate and read as many as you can find for style and format. I omit them to underscore the uniqueness of each funding source and each grant proposal you write. The surest ways to ensure your request will be denied are to (1) mail out form letters shotgun style, and (2) cut and paste paragraphs from a variety of generic samples. Even though the actual writing of the proposal is a small part of the overall process, it may be the most difficult to do well since it is imperative that it be original, unique, and in your own words.

- **Unintended but inevitable bias** will seep in because I live in Southern California and my clients are primarily small nonprofit organizations in human services. I talk and correspond with many people in other fields, subscribe to dozens of blogs, and surf the web daily for information about what is happening in other fields and other parts of the country, but you may frequently need to compensate if you're in biomedical research in the Deep South.

- **Activities** are listed at the end of each chapter rather than the tests often found in other books in the Demystified series. Grant writing is a process rather than a body of information and actually taking the steps to collect and refine material to create a functional grant proposal seems more relevant to me than checking to see if you know the difference between public and private foundations or how many billions of dollars the federal government allocates to research each year.

- The **Glossary** is huge but not exhaustive. I've used vernacular definitions as much as possible and included variations of common terms. Funders change jargon as fast as teenagers, however, so don't consider the Glossary the final word.

- The **Resource List** is also lengthy and contains only a smidgeon of the books, blogs, web sites, consultants, and other helps on the Internet and in real life. Again, many of these resources change rapidly so the links I provide may not be in operation. Usually, if you use a few key words in your favorite search engine, you will be able to track them down or find a similar site.

I arranged all my source material in alphabetical order at the back of the book rather than adding footnotes to the text, printing smaller bibliographies at the end of each chapter, or even organizing it by categories. Some of my reasons for doing this are:

1. A single sentence or paragraph may contain information from two or three sources but my University of Chicago training makes me acknowledge every single document I consulted even if I used only the whiff of an idea or a single statistic that can be found in a dozen other places.

2. Some resources like The Foundation Center, The Grantsmanship Center, and Grants.gov could be listed in almost every category I devised—and

some like Western Carolina University or San Bernardino County Grants Office don't quite fit anywhere.

3. Specific information may be of vital importance to one reader and almost useless to another, so I'm not going to be the one to make that judgment call. If a blogger I think is great turns you off, don't subscribe.

4. A wealth of material on grant writing exists in the most unlikely places and I want you to enjoy the rich cross-fertilization of ideas that comes from a random juxtaposition of references.

My final quirk resides with the phrase *grant writer*. Since the job of preparing a proposal for funding entails so many more tasks than writing, the label *grant writer* seems an inappropriate attempt to both elevate and discount the work we do. Certainly, for convenience sake or to fill out a form, I call myself a grant writer, but I don't use that term when I speak to myself or people who matter to me. I advise you to follow suit. You are learning to be a grant professional—you are preparing proposals to obtain grant funds for a special project—you are a fundraiser who specializes in grants; there are dozens of ways to describe what you and I are doing. Find one that fits better than "grant writer"—and remind me gently when I forget. Thank you.

And Now for Content

Chapter 1: *Exploring Grantsmanship Basics*—We'll look at some of the common assumptions about grants and separate what is fact and what is fiction.

Chapter 2: *Defining Your Project*—You'll create wish lists of things you want money for through several individual and group activities that look at program designs from several different perspectives.

Chapter 3: *Creating a Budget*—First comes the program design, and then comes a consideration of the money you'll need to implement it. You'll focus on realistic expenses that tie activities to be funded by potential grants to the resources and mission of the agency.

Chapter 4: *Proving the Need*—In this chapter, you'll concentrate on determining and demonstrating the importance and impact of the proposed projects to the community and world rather than focus on the needs of your particular agency.

Chapter 5: *Establishing Your Credibility*—Next you'll explore ways to demonstrate that you and your agency are capable of handling the grant responsibly and that your project is a wise use of the funder's money.

Chapter 6: *Considering Ethical Issues*—You'll use the Code of Ethics adopted by the Association of Fundraising Professionals to explore some of the ethical challenges you might face in writing a proposal.

Chapter 7: *Refining Your Program Design*—You'll expand your project list from Chapter 2 to include specific details on what you are proposing to do, who is going to do it, and how you will measure the project's success. A large part of this chapter deals with the importance of working with partners in collaborative efforts.

Chapter 8: *Focusing on Foundations*—You'll learn the different kinds of grants and foundations and how to find them.

Chapter 9: *Demystifying Government Funding*—You'll investigate city, county, and state funding sources that are close to home and relatively easy to obtain before exploring Grants.gov and the 26 federal agencies that make research and other substantial multiyear grants.

Chapter 10: *Cultivating Corporate and Individual Gifts*—You'll learn to identify and tap individual donors, smaller grants from regional business firms, and in-kind contributions of products and services.

Chapter 11: *Reading Guidelines and RFPs*—You'll examine every word of the printed instructions to see if your project is eligible, decode jargon to determine exactly what the funder wants, and find ways to get additional information about funding sources.

Chapter 12: Writing the Narrative—Finally! Now that you have all the information collected, it's time to start writing letters of intent (LOIs) and filling in the blanks of a variety of application forms.

Chapter 13: *Submitting Your Proposal*—You'll scrutinize your work to make sure nothing has been left out and that other people can read and understand your proposal. Most importantly, you'll meet the deadline with time to spare.

Chapter 14: *Following Up and Starting Over*—You'll learn what to do when you get the grant, what to do if you don't get what you requested, and what to do while you're waiting to hear.

While there is a logical order to the work outlined in the chapters, the process is not nearly as organized in actual practice. Tasks overlap, stacks of paper threaten to take over your entire office, and nothing seems to fit together. Don't panic. Everything will eventually come together and make sense. By the end of the book, you'll have at least one proposal ready to refine for the dozen or more funding sources you have identified and researched. While there is no guarantee that they will be funded, the probability will be very high since they will be unique, passionate, and professionally prepared—and you'll be ready to start all over again with new needs and ideas.

Final Words

The grant-writing world changes as quickly as a small boy outgrows his shoes. Acronyms for government programs are changing and federal departments are considering different funding priorities as I write. Some of the resources I've listed will have left the scene and new ones will be available by the time this book is printed. I trust you will take those errors in good stride. If, however, I have omitted something important, garbled information, gotten some facts wrong, or if I've confused you, I take full responsibility and want to know about it. Please contact me at maryann@paynecns.com so I can change that section when we update the book.

Thank you in advance for the passion and dedication that drives you to consider submitting grant proposals to fund a valuable project that is central to your life. Together, we *can* make our corners of the world richer, wiser, and more humane for ourselves and those around us.

chapter 1

Exploring Grantsmanship Basics

The man on top of the mountain does not fall there.

Chinese Fortune Cookie

Ofelia teaches third grade in an inner-city school with a large immigrant population. She asks each child to read aloud to their families every night for 20 minutes. Recently three parents have shyly thanked her and admitted they don't read English as well as their children. They read too well to enroll in the literacy program at the library but not well enough to help their children when they stumble with a word. One mother said she was afraid she didn't always understand the information that came with medicines for her child's asthma and asked Ofelia to read it for her. Another mother asked if she would consider teaching parents how to help their children with homework. Ofelia would love to do this, but she'll need teaching materials, training for herself, and money for child care if this is going to be an ongoing project. Her classroom budget has no money for programs like this, and she doesn't want to charge the parents. Maybe she can get a grant to at least try out the idea.

Michelle is a pre-med student interested in finding ways to help her grandmother who is having increasing difficulty moving around because of her arthritis. Michelle is not sure if she wants to go into research or clinical work, but she's being encouraged by a favorite faculty member to write a grant proposal and explore some options.

Boyd is a junior faculty member at a land grant college; he wants to establish a small but significant place for himself. He concentrated on corn breeding in graduate school, but an infestation of corn borers played havoc with some of his experiments. Now he's wondering if he should shift his focus a bit and concentrate on controlling or at least managing his enemy. To do that, he'll need to find money outside the department's current budget.

You and thousands of other people like Ofelia, Michelle, and Boyd have both personal and professional reasons for considering writing an application for a grant. You may have some reservations about your chances of getting money this way, but a persistent project that needs funding keeps swimming just outside your consciousness. You've seen the ads that promise easy money, and you're more than skeptical about their promises. You may have heard that grant writing is difficult, and you wonder if you have the skills that are needed. In spite of these hesitations, however, you've decided it's time to at least explore the idea of finding a grant to underwrite a project that is important to you.

Congratulations! You've taken two important steps toward writing a successful grant proposal.

1. You have a passion for solving a problem, helping someone else, or filling a gap in either services or knowledge that won't go away.

2. You are looking for a guide because you know this is new territory that shifts quickly, and you want to follow basic steps without any false promises.

As you browse, and later read this book and complete the suggested activities, your passion will be needed to complete the myriad small, but time-consuming tasks that are part of the proposal-writing process. Your idea will become the kernel of a research or social service project that forms the core element in seeking and receiving a grant award.

Let's start with some of the common assumptions and misperceptions about the whole field of grantsmanship. We'll concentrate on fleshing out your ideas in Chapter 2.

Anyone Can Write a Grant Proposal

This is true. If you are comfortable with a computer, can organize your thoughts in writing, know how to follow directions, and are patient, you have the basic skills needed for completing a funding request. It helps if you're curious, able to work under tight deadlines, and have access to a copy of Adobe Acrobat Suite (the expensive version), which is helpful in filling out the increasing numbers of online submissions.

Anyone Can Receive a Grant

This is *not* true. The vast majority of grants are reserved for nonprofit organizations, including colleges and universities, school districts, medical and research centers, youth groups, and other community-based agencies. You'll hear and read the phrase "proof of 501(c)(3) status" until you want to scream. This IRS tax-exempt designation is required by most funders. In addition, each foundation and government entity has detailed guidelines on who can receive funds and for what purposes they are to be spent. We'll explore how to decide whether you are eligible for specific funds or not in Chapter 11. For now, let's look at broad groups of people and their relative chances for obtaining a grant.

- Faith-based organizations are now eligible for many federal and foundation grants. This is a relatively recent development and more funds are available each year.

- The same holds true for private and charter schools—and individual teachers within schools.

- It's more difficult to get money if you're an individual. Limited funds are available for writers, photographers, musicians, and others in the fine arts, and for research purposes for people connected with a university, medical center, or research institute. Money also exists for individual scholarships and fellowships, which are not technically considered grants but follow a very similar application pattern. Many self-employed people enter into a partnership with a nonprofit organization to do a joint project.

- There are even fewer grant funds available for small business firms. Contrary to the ubiquitous ads, the federal government does *not* provide money for starting or expanding a business. Contracts are available, however, through state and local governments for such things as expanding child-care centers, creating energy-efficient technology, retraining unemployed workers, as well as for specialized research and other forms of economic development. In addition, the Small Business Administration (www.sba.gov) provides a variety of loans for small, women-owned, and minority business firms. Finally, governments at all levels procure products and services through a bidding process. Each of these funding streams requires documents that have some similarities to the grant proposals this book covers.

- If you are a charity, but do not have 501(c)(3) status, you will need to immediately apply to the IRS and your state's attorney general. Information about how to do this is covered in Chapter 5.

- Finally, if you have less than three years' experience as an organization or have not received a research grant on your own, chances of foundation and/or government money are very slim. Chapter 10 offers some options to explore, but it's wise to know that the odds are stacked against you.

Grants Are a Fast Way to Get Money

This is *not true*! Obtaining a grant is probably the slowest way to raise money you can imagine. If you've forgotten to fill in all the blanks, missed the deadline, or committed another obvious error, you may get a postcard within a week or two saying your proposal has been denied. Otherwise, you'll wait until the foundation board or review panel acts before you hear anything. Many foundation boards meet quarterly so it will be three to four months at the earliest before you hear from them. Federal and state governments are notoriously slow. Even after the award has been made, contracts must be negotiated and signed before you receive a check. Some government grants, especially in social services and mental health, reimburse you *after* you have performed the services.

Grant Writing Is Simply Filling in a Form

This is F-A-L-S-E in capital letters. Although that is sometimes the last step in applying for funds, writing is the smallest part of preparing a grant proposal. My first Head Start proposal took more than 200 hours to prepare. Now I estimate a proposal for a new client or a government grant will still take between 75 and 80 hours. That's because there's a lot more to asking for a grant than the writing. Even the one-page ads that promise an easy path to fast cash list several steps in the process. As the chapters in this book demonstrate, the basic parts of "writing a grant" include:

- Defining a fundable project
- Demonstrating a need for the project and justifying its expense

- Showing that you or your group is the appropriate agent to implement the research or program
- Refining the proposal with details of objectives, activities, staffing, partners, and evaluation
- Researching and prioritizing funding sources
- Creating a realistic budget that supports the goals of the project
- Writing the narrative
- Preparing a presentation that meets the funder's requirements

It's wise to estimate your first submission for a major grant will take a minimum of three months and may require even more time if critical elements are not in place. For example, if you have a clear picture of projects you want to fund, have a reputable connection with potential collaborators, and have identified a handful of funding sources, two months may be enough to prepare a letter of intent or a simple proposal. If, however, you've operated solo up until now, have no idea of how many teens will show up for a drumming workshop, or haven't done a literature search to see how many other people are working in nanotech drug delivery, you'll want considerably more time to collect the information and connections you need.

Grants Are Free Money

This is another false statement. In addition to the energy, time, and miscellaneous expenses involved in securing grant funds, all grants come with strings attached.

- First, you have to use the money in the manner spelled out in your request. If you write in your narrative that you will use the money to add music, art, and writing experiences to a senior nutrition program, you can't use the funds to repair the roof when it leaks. Similarly, if you receive money for roof repairs and you find someone to donate time and materials to do the job, you can't use the funds to pay the receptionist's salary. Occasionally, you can negotiate a budget adjustment but it is usually limited to a 10 percent variation and requires serious negotiations and approvals.
- A corollary is that grant funds must be segregated in separate accounts with rigorous attention to accounting procedures and strict adherence to the approved budget. The penalty for playing loose with funds is the very

real possibility that you will need to return the entire grant, including money already spent, when the irregularities are discovered.

- Record-keeping and reporting is often more complex when a grant is involved than when the funds come from other sources. People who attend a golf tournament are content to know their money goes to provide swimming lessons and summer camps for low-income kids. Your board wants to know if the grant covered the cost of the swimming and camp as predicted. A foundation is interested in how many kids took swimming lessons, how many attended camp, and how many more kids learned to swim or went to camp because of their contribution. The federal government will ask how many unduplicated kids between the ages of five and twelve attended six or more swimming lessons, what specific skills they gained, and how their new self-confidence and friendships had an impact on the level of violence at summer camp. This is not a particularly good example, but you get the idea and can use your imagination to see similar levels of reporting for research projects.

- Many costs will not be covered by grant funds. Some you may know about in advance, such as administrative overhead, the annual audit, or the agreed-upon matching funds. Some may appear because you forgot to include something in the budget, and some will occur because situations change. Unless you're very careful, your grant can cost you more money than you expected.

Grant Money Will Sustain Your Program

The answer to this statement is yes and no. While some child-care, mental health, juvenile justice, substance abuse, and research programs rely heavily on government grants, it's unwise to count on grant funds or government contracts to operate your entire agency or research effort. You probably can't even make a significant dent in a major project with grants. It doesn't matter whether your award is $500, $50,000 or $5 million, you will need funds to supplement any money you receive from grants to implement your proposal.

Why? Reasons include:

- Grants are awarded for specific activities for a specific period of time. They have a beginning and an end. Although an increasing number of grants are made for three to five years, most awards are for a single year. Sometimes you can reapply each year. Most often, you can't.

- Individuals, foundations, and government agencies like to see you have a strong enough commitment to your project to garner and invest local resources in its success. People who give money to others like to be partners, not sugar daddies.

- All funders report receiving many more requests than they can fund. The ratio varies from foundation to foundation and even between programs within government departments. In 2005, the National Institutes of Allergies and Infectious Diseases (NIAID) that is part of the National Institute of Health (NIH) received 43,069 applications and was able to fund 23.3 percent of them. If you do the math, you'll realize over 33,000 proposals were rejected. As more people apply and less money is available, this kind of percentage is becoming increasingly common. To stretch the money as far as it will go, some funders will also give you less than you requested so they can support more organizations and projects.

- Even if you receive everything you ask for, you are responsible for sustaining the project after the grant funds expire. Just as it's easier to find a new job while you're still employed, it's easier to raise money when you don't need it for survival.

- Most importantly, funders want to give away money. They don't want to conduct research or provide direct services themselves. They want to help many groups working in a field that advances their mission rather than operate a lab or agency on their own.

We'll look briefly at ways to efficiently and effectively gather additional funds in Chapters 8 and 10. In the meantime, keep an eye open for ways to address this fact of life. Now let's look at two assumptions that are a bit more subtle.

Grant Writers Speak Their Own Language

Again, this is a true *and* false statement. Every field has its own language that quickly becomes jargon. Grant writing is no exception. If you are a purist, you don't write grants. You write proposals *for* grants. A grant is money given for a specific purpose that doesn't need to be repaid. Those of us who "write grants" don't print the checks or even sign them. We define a project, collect appropriate materials to justify the need, and write an application requesting the awarding of that money. We "propose" opportunities for a foundation, corporation, or government agency to give away its funds.

There is an extensive glossary at the back of the book, and Chapter 9 lists abbreviations for government divisions that make grants. Since I don't use abbreviations when I write a proposal, I try not to use them in the book. A few acronyms and some unfamiliar words are sure to creep in, however. To aid your reading, here is some of the most frequently used jargon I share with other grant seekers, philanthropists, and the government, listed in the approximate order of frequency with which you'll hear and eventually use them yourself.

- **RFP**—Request for Proposal. This is the formal, printed announcement in the Federal Register that describes federal government funds that are open for applications. Over the years, it has become synonymous with any notice of available funds from all levels of the government and public and private foundations. Since all the rules and regulations for a particular grant are contained in this single document, the RFP will be your indispensible guide to applying for each grant. Also, because people can't leave a good thing alone, a host of variations have appeared. RFA (Request for Funding Assistance), NOFA (Notice of Funding Availability), SGA (Solicitation for Grant Applications), FFO (Federal Funding Opportunity), and FOA (Funding Opportunity Announcement) are a few current ones.

- **NPO**—Nonprofit Organization. Databases of funding sources and brief announcements of RFPs often abbreviate the types of organizations that can apply for funds.

  - **AVO**—All Volunteer Organization

  - **CBO**—Community-Based Organization. Sometimes the same as an NPO; sometimes AVOs, FBOs, and NPOs grouped together

  - **FBO**—Faith-Based Organization

  - **LEA**—Local Education Agency. Usually a school district or county office of education

  - **IHE**—Institution of Higher Education. Colleges, universities, trade schools

- **501(c)(3)**—Section of the IRS code that designates an organization as charitable and tax exempt. The vast majority of foundations require grant recipients to be 501(c)(3) organizations.

- **LOI**—Letter of Intent. A brief, often one-page, letter summarizing your grant request that is increasingly requested as a preliminary screening step by foundations. Since it's often difficult to write a summary before you have written the entire proposal, an LOI requires all the planning and decisions regarding a project are in place before you send it.

- **Program Office.** A staff member of a government agency, foundation, or corporate-giving program who administers the application process. This is usually the person who has practical answers to questions about a funding opportunity you are researching.

- **Collaborators.** Partners who have come together from different organizations or disciplines to work on a mutually beneficial project or program. The vast majority of government grants require some form of collaboration, and once again, foundations are following the trend. Members can include public and private organizations, government agencies, and individuals. In Chapters 2 and 7, we'll explore a variety of possible partnership arrangements

- **Sustainability**. The expectation that ongoing funds to continue the research or project will be raised from other sources when the grant expires. Both government and foundation applications often ask for a sustainability plan.

- **Logic Model.** A process that visually depicts assumptions and elements of a specific program. It can be as simple as describing the situation, inputs, outputs, and outcomes in chart form, or as elaborate as a circular flowchart with goals, resources, activities, outputs, and outcomes.

- **MOU**—Memorandum of Understanding. Legal document spelling out what the lead agency/principal investigator and each collaborating group or individual will and will not do to implement the proposal

You Can't Apply for a Grant Alone

There are two ideas contained in this heading, and both are true. First, preparing a grant proposal is a team effort. It's important that one person do the actual writing for continuity and completeness, but you'll need support from other staff collecting the needed information, and developing a realistic budget, and you'll need buy-in and approval from your governing board. If a school district, college, university, hospital, or research lab will be the official body receiving the grant, there will be a designated chain of command to create, review, and give approval to the final proposal. Establishing and cultivating relationships throughout your organization are important from the very beginning.

The second meaning of the heading refers to the evidence of partnerships with other researchers or agencies that an increasing number of funding sources require. In this book, I'm working on the premise that all grant requests will be collaborative in nature. If you want funds to add nutritional education to an existing food pantry, you need to know staff at the local WIC (a federally funded food supplement and support program for Women, Infants, and Children), have at least a nodding acquaintance with school, hospital, and senior food service personal, and be familiar with the churches, temples, and other groups that also distribute food and clothing. If you're seeking research funds, partners can be in other institutions or in other departments. Boyd, the corn breeder mentioned at the start of the chapter, will probably want to consult with an entomologist to learn more about his corn borers, a toxicologist to develop an effective kill agent, an engineer to produce an effective delivery system for the insecticide, and local authorities for permission to spray or otherwise kill the nasty bugs. It's a huge plus for your grant application if you can work together on the proposed new project. Yes, this adds time and complexity to your project, but it also adds depth, avoids duplication, and hopefully is more effective in meeting your long-term goals—and it increases your chances for receiving grants.

ACTIVITIES

1. Identify three or more assumptions you have made about the grant-writing process. Research what is true and false about each one.

2. Free-write three pages about what you hope to accomplish by receiving a grant. Condense that statement to one page. Further refine your purpose to one paragraph.

3. Identify which category of grant seeker you fit. What challenges do you expect to meet during the process of securing your first grant award?

4. Make two lists—one of things you need grant money for and the other things you already have or can find in other ways.

5. List jargon used in your field of interest. Spell out the words in acronyms and write a short definition for each word to explain it to someone outside your field.

6. Begin a list of people you can ask to help complete the grant proposal.

chapter 2

Defining Your Project

The best way to get a good idea is to get a lot of ideas.

Linus Pauling

You probably have a dozen ideas about how you could use grant money. That's good, because the first step of preparing a grant proposal is to dream. Now is the time to dream—and to start making lists. Refining your ideas into a few clearly defined projects that are feasible, realistic, and able to catch the imagination and dollars of foundation and government decision makers involves lists and more lists, meetings and more meetings, phone calls and more phone calls, and more writing than you can imagine. Not all of these steps are necessary for every grant proposal, but they are important to consider. If this is your first application, these steps are vital in laying a firm foundation for future funding. Shortcuts taken now are like speeding on the freeway. You may save a few seconds but end up twisted around a light pole.

Mind Mapping Your Dream Ideas

To begin, toss ideas around in your head for several days while you're carrying a small pad of paper and a pen in your pocket. Every time you're between activities, think of your project. Jot down your questions, your ideas, people

13

who might help, and variations on the theme as they occur to you. Don't worry about order or grammar or sentence structure. It's particularly important not to wonder if the jottings will be used or not. This single-person brainstorming is simply to get the creative juices flowing.

If you want to end homelessness, your list might start something like this:

Accurate census

Cure for mental illness

Tents

Locked storage spaces

Jobs

Ending isolation

Affordable housing

Empty buildings

Demographics

School for homeless kids

Rainwear

Blankets

Causes of homelessness

Attachment to pets

Cooking facilities

Showers

Transportation

Social workers

Computerized tracking

Health care

Budgeting help

Homeless veterans

Transitional housing

Counseling

First and last month rent fund

City ordinance changes

Current programs

When you have a list of 15 or 20 items, set aside an hour to do some **mind mapping** on a larger piece of paper. I like 11-inch by 17-inch because once I get started I have lots to write, but 8½-inch by 11-inch paper will work if you turn it sideways. It's also possible to download free mind mapping software from the Internet, but I find the kinesthetic sensation of pen to paper is more productive and more creative. You can experiment to see which method works best for you.

Start with a one- or two-word label for your project in a circle in the middle of the page. Let your mind wander just as it does while you're waiting at a stoplight. Each time a word or idea appears, write it down and draw a circle (or oval) around it. Connect it with a line to the word circle that prompted the thought. You'll end up with a coral reef kind of creature like the one I did for the expansion of a music academy.

Mind Map

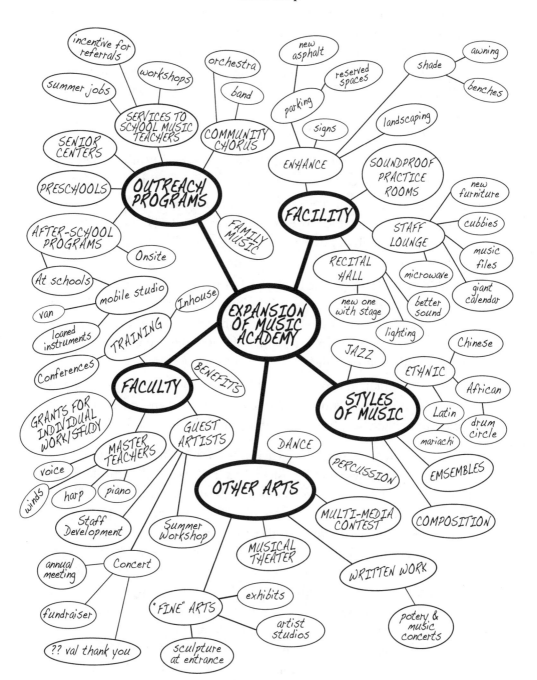

It's okay to use things from the little notebook you've been carrying around if you remember them, but don't peek at it yet. If you have lots of thoughts, your pen will be flying. If your ideas are sparse, write them down anyway and wait patiently for sprouts to appear. They will. Once again, this is a single-person method of the familiar brainstorming process you've probably done a million times, but don't scoff, it works—and you'll be sorry later if you skip this step now.

Just to remind you of brainstorming rules:

- **Don't judge or evaluate.** Just write—or draw—or add embellishments to your circles, but keep the pen moving. You can cross things off later.

- **Be creative.** Don't limit yourself to what is feasible or affordable or even possible. Dream about what you'd like to see happen. Add metaphors and feelings, colors and sounds. Flights of fantasy are allowed. In fact, they are encouraged.

- **Don't organize.** Just let one image lead to another. If the lines circle back, that's okay. If they cross, or produce long strings of disjointed thoughts, that's okay, too. If all of the "balloons" connect to the central circle, however, it's time to stand up, get a drink of water, then come back and start on one of the outlying ideas.

- **Don't overthink.** Draw pictures if that's what you see. Add slogans, puns, symbols, secret jokes. You want this to be a source of energy for later work, so keep it playful and fun. Use both hemispheres of your brain.

Keep your pen moving until the page is filled or until you reach that "ah ha" moment when you know you're finished. You'll recognize that subtle shift in thinking that says, "I'm done for today. I know the path I want to follow." That's the time to put your mind map in a safe place and take the next step.

After a break, summarize your project focus in a single phrase of less than 10 words. You will use this phrase as a *purpose statement* to explain your project to other people as you gather more information for your program design. Keep it broad, but make it a little more specific than your first idea. For example, instead of "end homelessness," your new focus might be "provide support services to homeless families" or "turn an empty building into a shelter for homeless veterans" or "conduct research on the causes of homelessness." On the other hand, you might simply change "expansion of music academy" to "expand music academy" to cast it in an active rather than passive mode or choose "expand outreach programs offered by music academy." Go with the idea that has the most energy and passion behind it.

Inviting Others to Join You

It's time for the first of several reality checks. You will not be doing this project by yourself, so it's important to get other people's buy-in and ideas. Have you identified the problem correctly? Are the ideas you've generated the most important aspects of the problem to tackle? What have you forgotten? You need to ask these questions of someone other than yourself.

I know it's sometimes easier and faster to do things by yourself, but that won't fly in the grantsmanship world. Experienced grant professionals agree one of the most important elements in preparing a proposal is the connections you make. Not only are they important factors in checking the feasibility of your project, expanding the number and type of implementation strategies, and making sure you include the important elements, but funders place a high premium on your ability to demonstrate collaborative efforts in both the planning and implementation of your project. This has become even more important in a time of decreasing funds from traditional sources and increased competition from newcomers to your field.

People you consult will vary depending on whether you are proposing a community service or embarking on a research project. The chart below shows the kinds of people you might want to consider.

People to Consult	
Community Service Project	**Research Project**
President and members of board of directors	Department chair and principal investigator
Program staff	Colleagues at home institutions
Current clients/program participants	People who will benefit from study
"Alumni" of similar programs	Colleagues in related fields of study
Potential program participants	Colleagues in tangential and non-related fields
Colleagues from other social service agencies	Colleagues at other institutions
College professors in related fields of study	Community members interested in subject
Community leaders	Representative from grants office
Support staff in accounting, clerical, custodial	Support staff like lab technicians, IT, clerical
Vendors	Vendors

You will probably think of other categories to add as you make your own chart with specific names to replace the generic titles so by all means, do so.

To get useful feedback from others, it's important to ask the right people the right questions in the right context. It would be foolish to include everyone in one giant meeting so let's spend a little time looking at settings and approaches for different groups.

Questorming with Key People

Let's go back a step and examine the basic questions and problems your project is addressing by asking questions like those raised earlier when you were refining a purpose statement. **Questorming** is a variation of brainstorming developed at MIT in the 1950s that focuses on asking questions rather than seeking solutions. If your proposed project is broad and somewhat fuzzy (and it should be at this point), questions like those below will help you develop a more concise, focused problem formulation.

- What are the best questions we should be asking in order to do this project?
- What should we ask to determine whether or not this project should be undertaken?
- What do we need to ask to evaluate the impact of this project?
- What are likely to be the consequences of implementing this project?
- Are we lacking critical information before proceeding further? If so, how can we get it?
- What cross-disciplinary skills and information would be useful in conducting this research?
- Who are the stakeholders? How do we include them in meaningful ways?
- Have we covered all the major possibilities? Are we overlooking anything?

Gather two or three people who are key to the success of your project. If you are the executive director of a community agency, you might invite the board president and/or appropriate committee chair, the advisory committee chair, and the program director or a key staff member already working in this field. If you are considering a research project, choose people in your own and related departments who have the experience and skills you will need. If this is a thesis project, ask your committee. Send an invitation memo that invites them to a 30- to 40-minute session to consider the questions you need to ask about the proposal focus from your mind map. If your office is too small to meet comfortably, reserve a conference room. Ask a friend or clerical support person to be your recorder and you're all set. You can either ask the questions yourself to guide the discussion or enlist the help of your advisor or a facilitator but your main role is to listen.

Remember this is queststorming, so focus on eliciting questions rather than answers. The results of the meeting should be another list of questions. Here are some that came from asking the question: *"What are the best questions we need to ask to provide support services for unemployed residents in our community?"*

- What services are currently provided by the state, county, community colleges, and other agencies?
- What kinds of jobs are available? For unskilled workers? For high school graduates? For seniors? For people with an arrest record?
- What are the characteristics of people who are unemployed? Of discouraged workers?
- What job search skills are most effective?
- Who is providing job training?
- What skills do previously employed workers have? Those who have never been employed? What new skills do they need?
- What barriers exist for job seekers? Transportation? Relevant skills? Uniforms or professional clothing? Child care? Other?

If the questions expand your list of things to do, that's okay. The process will help refine and make the finished program design sharper and more realistic. For a sense of closure, however, you might finish with questions like:

- Is the research question I'm asking answerable?
- Have the questions underlying the proposed project been addressed?
- Are we asking the best questions for this stage of the proposal process?
- What kind of resources do we have within this group? Time? Space? Information? Skills? Materials? What do we need?

Finish the session with a brief recap of the main questions that have emerged, thank the participants for their time and assistance, and promise to keep them in the loop as you move forward. Within the next couple of days, transcribe and condense the questions that were generated into a one-page document. Send this sheet to each person at the meeting with another note of thanks. File the back-up material because you will want to use some of the details in your proposal. Keep the summary handy, however, to serve as a road map for the work you will be doing in the next few weeks.

Focusing on Concepts

Some people are visual and think in graphic terms while others prefer more linear forms so **concept mapping** is a great tool because it speaks to both groups. The technique was developed by Joseph D. Novak and his research team at Cornell University in the 1970s to organize emerging interdisciplinary scientific knowledge for students and faculty. It's a variation of mind mapping that begins with a concept rather than a word and is a bit more hierarchical in structure. The emphasis is on showing the relationship between concepts rather than generating questions or solutions. Linking phrases such as "gives rise to," "results in," "is required by," "with," "includes," etc., show how one idea leads to another, which is tied to third, which connects back to the first. Creating a concept map works well with the information suggested in questorming and is a useful step in determining how to implement your proposed project because it represents both time sequence and the interrelatedness of partners and activities.

You can create a concept map by yourself or include a few people with program or research knowledge related to your project. This is a good activity to engage colleagues in your department or from related agencies, as well as interested and knowledgeable outsiders. Follow the organizational steps you used for questorming to gather six or eight people together to develop a concept map that looks something like the one on the next page that explores the eradication of pine beetles.

The best way to facilitate the group process using this technique is to say one of the linking phrases out loud immediately after the recorder writes down a concept. You can follow that stream for a while by repeating the same linking word or phrase. Then return to the original concept and provide a different linking word or phrase and see where that leads. Draw the arrows in the original direction the process takes. When you discover the connection flowing backward, use different words on the other side of a double-tipped arrow or add a new arrow going in the opposite direction. Soon you'll have connections between several concepts, and you may discover the one you started is in the middle

Concept Map

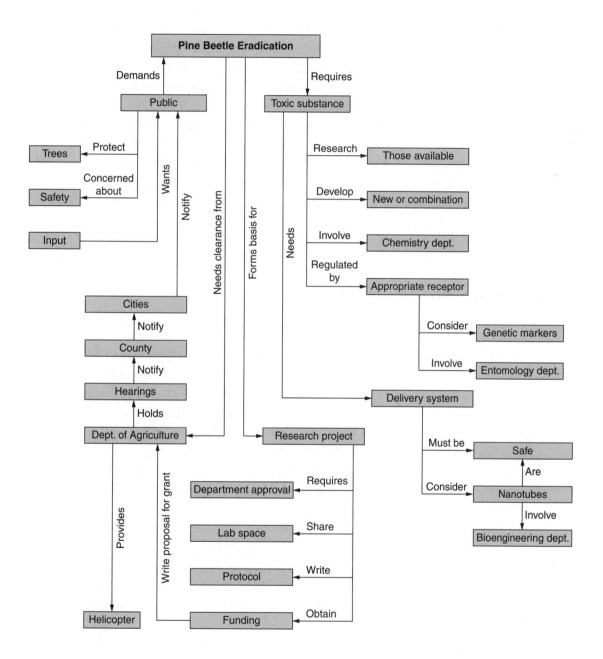

of a maze. You may also discover more people to contact and include in your project as your concept map begins to take on a life of its own. This is good because it's easy to forget that a tutorial program needs janitors, as well as reading material, or that adding new signs to a music academy might need a city permit. It's also smarter and easier to remember to notify people you will be spraying their mountain cabin for bark beetles before you do so rather than dealing with the media and their outrage afterwards.

Once again, after you thank the people for coming, you need to create a picture like the one shown on pine beetles and send it with a second thank-you. Software is available to create concept maps, but because this is a working document, you can chose to simply hand-draw one on 11- by 17-inch paper for your own use and reduce it to 8½- by 11-inch for distribution. Finally, don't forget to keep the comments and tangents for reference later. This project may still take several twists and turns.

Brainstorming with People Who Know

You may think you know what research should be done or how a human service project should be structured, but the real people who know are those who will reap the benefits of your proposal and those who have conducted similar projects. Your next task will be to gather a sizeable group of those people and hold a brainstorming session to generate and record even more ideas about your preliminary project idea. Because the rules are simple and familiar and the process is fun, brainstorming can be used effectively in a large, disparate group of people who may not know each other. It's messy sometimes, but again, the information you gather will be invaluable for a winning proposal and an effective project.

Choose people you identified as program staff, current clients, "alumni," potential program participants, colleagues in related or complementary fields of work, support staff, vendors, and community members who have an interest in your field. You'll want at least 12 to15 people, so invite 30–40. Include people who surfaced in the questorming because this time you will be looking for:

- Potential partners
- Elements to add or subtract from your initial project design
- Barriers and gaps that need attention

- Community resources to augment your project
- History of what does and doesn't work locally and in other communities
- Perceived benefits of your proposed effort
- Community supporters
- Prospective funding streams

By now you know the steps of holding a productive meeting, but let me add a few additional suggestions because this will be a larger group and you'll need to be a bit more organized.

- Phone, email, or otherwise personally invite each person. Follow up a verbal invitation with a written notice that includes the estimated time (90 minutes for this group) and purpose of the meeting.

- Reserve a room and arrange for a recorder. If you have invited 40 people, set up the room for 30 and have spare chairs handy. It's better to have every chair filled than to have large empty rows or a single person at a table with eight chairs. You also want everyone to participate easily so if you expect more than a dozen, arrange for two recorders and/or someone to tape the session.

- Plan to have some kind of refreshments. You are building relationships, as well as gathering information, so prepare as if you are inviting people to your home. If you serve coffee, make arrangements for tea, add bottled water to a selection of soft drinks, and show that you are attentive to individual differences by your choice of food.

- People may not know each other (so nametags will probably be appropriate) and they will undoubtedly arrive at different times so I suggest you begin with the kind of flexible, interactive activities that Eva Schindler-Rainman called "raggedy beginnings." Start a graffiti wall and invite people to respond to posted words and phrases or build a group mind map surrounding your proposed project. Pass out forms for people to interview someone to introduce later. Even do a silly party ice breaker that can be easily stopped when most of the group has arrived.

- Thank everyone for coming. Remind them of the purpose of the meeting (to help the agency collect ideas and resources about XYZ). If the raggedy beginning didn't involve interviewing someone else, ask everyone to introduce themselves and answer one specific question related to the topic of the day. (*Give your name, agency or job title, and one service that would make life better for homeless/elderly/young people in our community. Or, tell us how you would benefit if we expanded the music academy.*)

- Restate the purpose and expectations of the meeting once again and review or teach the four basic guidelines for brainstorming:

  - Criticism is ruled out.

  - Freewheeling ideas are welcome.

  - Quantity is wanted.

  - Combination and improvement are sought.

- Decide which of the eight possible outcomes (potential partners; additions or subtractions from your project design; barriers and gaps; community resources; history of what does and doesn't work; desired benefits; community supporters; and prospective funding streams) you want to elicit through group process and which you want to collect through personal observation.

- You may want to brainstorm more than one question, but limit the number to three. If you used the graffiti wall as a raggedy beginning, start with one of those topics and add suggestions. Look at the questions from the questorming session to see which ones might be applicable.

- Expect a pause after a rush of ideas. Be patient and give people permission to dig deeper for comments they think are silly or impractical. You'll find someone brave enough to make a suggestion—and then the ball will get rolling again.

- If there is time and you want help in setting priorities, ask people to rank the suggestions that have been made. An easy way to do this if ideas are posted on newsprint around the room is to give each person three colored stickers to affix to the three suggestions they think have the most merit, should be implemented first, or another ranking criteria you select. If ideas were taped or are not easily accessible, distribute half sheets of brightly colored paper and ask people to list three answers to the ranking question you raise. (Brightly colored paper is as an important ingredient as the choice of refreshments, since it's another detail that says you put time and energy into planning this day and you will find and appreciate the feedback they provide.)

- Ten minutes before you said the meeting would end, ask if there are any final comments, summarize the main contributions, and thank everyone for coming. Stand by the door to say thank-you and good-bye to everyone as they leave.

- Clean up and transcribe the notes. Condense them to one page and send them with a thank-you note to everyone who attended. Also send them with a note to the people who didn't attend saying you missed them and wonder if they have anything to add to the group's feedback.

Creating Order from Chaos

Before you forget what everybody suggested and offered, you'll need to establish some kind of organizational system. What did you learn from listening to all those people? Are there changes you'd like to make in your original project vision?

Sort all of the suggestions you've collected into four lists: NOW, LATER, MUCH LATER, and NEVER:

- The NOW list will be activities you can start immediately with or without grant money. Do so, and keep track of what you're doing to include in the narrative section to demonstrate you're able to handle the proposed project. Consider equipment, staff, facilities, and support services you can use to expand or continue the new activities and those that will need additional money. For example, you can begin a weekly walking program for seniors with a volunteer coordinator and request grants to purchase exercise tapes and minimal exercise aids like pool noodles or aerobic steps, train existing staff in physical fitness for aging adults, or develop an adaptive ethnic dance program.

- The LATER list is for ideas that need an infusion of money, time, and other resources. The senior program's beginning idea might have been to hire an instructor with experience in geriatric exercise or add a major piece of equipment like a resistance or elliptical chair to the exercise room. Combine the brainstorming suggestions into clusters for four or five grant proposals. Be sure to include projects you bumped from the NOW section.

- Items on the MUCH LATER list will either require large amounts of money or can happen only as a result of other actions to be taken first. If the senior center doesn't have a pool, asking for money for a water aerobics class doesn't make sense. Similarly, asking for funds to build a pool is not a good idea until you have a solid track record of successful grant applications and a thriving senior fitness program with a clear need for water activities for arthritic clients. Don't throw this list away, however, because you might find a partner who has a pool that is virtually unused during portions of the day or week and you can investigate a joint proposal.

- I try never to say never, but you need a NEVER list in this situation to contain ideas that are outside the boundaries of your agency's mission, your personal purpose, or any written short- and long-term goals. Remind yourself of the breadth but also the boundaries of your overall work. Now is not the time to go beyond those limits. If your primary focus is serving seniors, it might make sense to look at an intergenerational oral history project, a grandparents' reading hour at a library, or a prevention program dealing with the misuse of prescription drugs, but don't ask for funds to hold bike safety rodeos for preteens or establish a skateboarding program in hopes of attracting more family members. Don't chase after money just because it's available.

A second reason to judge something unacceptable is because of a known duplication of effort. For example, even if housing is a major need for the seniors you serve, when the city or private developers are constructing affordable apartment complexes and Habitat for Humanity has just announced they will focus on remodeling homes for the elderly for the next five years in your area, don't enter the housing arena. It's not only bad manners, but if you don't have the background in that area, you won't get the grant. Consider instead a joint effort where these other groups build the apartments and you provide onsite activities for the residents or transportation to meals and programs you already sponsor.

Finally, there are ethical reasons you may not want to accept funds from a specific funding source. For example, a substance abuse or domestic violence program might want to place foundations from corporations that produce alcoholic drinks on the NEVER list because alcoholism is a major contributing factor to the problem they are seeking to solve. Other ethical situations that might cause an idea to be rejected are explored in Chapter 6.

Patterns will emerge from the clusters of suggestions. Many will be refinements of your original idea. Some may lead to a companion project. If you run into trouble writing a new organizing purpose, try writing descriptive phrases in the present rather than future or declarative tense. "Expand wellness opportunities for seniors" becomes "Seniors are dancing the salsa in the multipurpose room while the Weekly Walkers leave for a two-mile hike to see spring flowers, widowers are learning to prepare one-pot meals in the kitchen, and a volunteer physical therapist is leading chair exercises in Room 3." Envisioning real people engaged in activities that grant funds will make possible often restores the original passion for the project and helps crystallize your thinking.

Exploring Who's Doing What

While you are meeting people in person, you also need to be searching the literature to find out what people are doing in your field in other parts of the world. This is especially true if you're planning a research or pilot project, but it applies in other areas as well. An increasing number of RFPs and foundation guidelines in education and social services ask for "research-based activities." What are best practices in gerontology? Where is cutting-edge research in pancreatic cancer being done? How are classroom teachers integrating comics and video games into English grammar lessons? The people who read and review your grant proposal will know at least a little from reading newspapers and listening to National Public Radio. They want you to educate them further and place your proposal in context.

Literature searches have gone online and have become increasingly specialized so we will not dwell on the details of how to conduct them. If you're already working in the field, start with the professional journals you already know and use. If you bought this book at a college bookstore or received it as a PDF for an online class, you have the skills and avenues to find relevant material to document the state of the art in your interest area. If your project involves K–12 education, speak to the district evaluator. If you purchased *Grant Writing Demystified* online or from another off-campus venue, go to the nearest college or university library and ask for help. It will be easier and faster to use specialized journals and search engines than to wander aimlessly on the Internet.

Looking for Partners

With competition for limited funds increasing, funders look most favorably on organizations and individuals who work collaboratively with others to avoid duplication and share resources. Collaborations can range from informal sharing of information as you have been doing during this research phase to formal agreements in which two or more individuals or agencies share space, program responsibility, or research activities. In addition to being a primary source of information about foundations, The Foundation Center (www.foundationcenter.org) has gathered a wealth of data on how nonprofit organizations can collaborate to achieve their missions. They list several ways agencies and individuals can collaborate including:

- Purchasing goods and/or services together
- Sharing space
- Combining marketing efforts
- Sharing staffing and/or staff training
- Sharing program development and delivery
- Sharing advocacy efforts

As you explore who is also addressing the problem you want to solve, keep your eyes open for people to include as partners in a joint effort. These might be people you invited to one of your brainstorming groups, an agency you discovered during your research process, someone you met at a community networking meeting, someone who has skills or other resources you need, or someone with whom you are already working. Meet with them individually to explore how a joint proposal might benefit both of you.

Sifting and Sorting the Ideas

Don't be in a rush to start writing a proposal immediately. Let the input from other people simmer for a few days. Sketch out a few program implementation designs. Where will your project take place? Who will be involved as participants? What kind of staffing will you need? Were any of the people involved in the group meetings potential partners for some aspect of the program? Are there individuals you want to talk to who weren't available earlier? Keep asking yourself questions and jotting down ideas. You have other research to do and documents to gather before you come back to the actual program development.

ACTIVITIES

1. Create a mind map to describe the project you want funded.

2. With the assistance of at least two key people, develop at least four key questions to answer about your project.

3. Identify 10 or more people or agencies to ask for feedback about your initial project idea.

4. Hold one or more small groups to gather ideas to incorporate into your project.

5. Experiment with two or more of the idea-gathering strategies presented in the chapter (solo brainstorming, group brainstorming, questorming, mind mapping, concept mapping).

6. Identify two or more potential partners for further discussions.

7. Conduct a literature search to discover the history, current best practices, and trends in your field. Write a one paragraph summary for each finding.

8. Sort the feedback you received for program design into NOW, LATER, MUCH LATER, and NEVER piles.

9. Sketch two or more ideas for potential proposals in phrases of eight to ten words.

10. Consider several potential partners for each potential proposal and begin exploratory conversations to see if working together is feasible and would bring strengths to your project.

chapter 3

Creating a Budget

In most workshops, classes, and books about grant writing, the budget is left to the end of the process as the last step before you submit your proposal. I've purposefully chosen to change that pattern, because *money matters*. You are asking for money, you want to find someone who has money to give you, and you need to convince that individual or foundation or government review board that you know enough about money to spend theirs wisely. Remember that one of the key questions grant makers ask is, "Are you the best person (agency) to do this project?" Showing you have a clear understanding of finances is one way—and an important way—to answer this question. Why should we leave as critical a topic as money to the end of our process? We won't!

One of the other reasons budget matters occur early in this book is to prevent you from committing one of my pet peeves and one of grantsmanship's major sins. All too often, I've had a client look at the range of previous grants from a foundation and say, "They give up to $50,000 so let's ask for the max." That's fine if that's what you need; otherwise it's greedy, and funders can tell the difference. You need to make budget decisions based on program needs and not because money might be available. Before you even start looking for sources of funds, it's important to decide how you are going to use the money and how much you really need.

Another reason to talk about budgets early in the process is that grant funds are designated money and need to be segregated from other accounts regardless of how large or small the amount is. If you are an individual, you will need to set up a separate checking account. If your project is part of an agency or organization, your accounting staff may be able to do this internally if it's a small grant for a limited and easily tracked purpose. In other situations, a separate banking account may be the easiest way to insure funds are not comingled. Your major concern as the grant writer is to create a separate budget and leave the logistics of managing how it is administered to others, just like you will be doing with program implementation. And, just like in program development, it's important that you understand enough about the field to provide the eventual staff with the tools (in this case, money) to do their job well.

Working Backward

The final budget may look something like the table below.

Income Sources	This Request	Total Project Budget	% of Project Income	Total Agency Budget	Project % of Total Income
Gov. Grants			5 %		
Foundation & Corp. Grants			55 %		
United Way			0		
Indiv. Contributions			10 %		
Earned Income			10 %		
Interest Income			0		
Fundraising Events (net)			10 %		
In-Kind Support			10 %		
Other Income			0		
TOTAL INCOME			100 %		
EXPENSES					
Personnel			25 %		
Benefits			5 %		
Total Personnel Costs			(30 %)		
Consultants			5 %		
Fundraising Expenses			0		
Supplies and Materials			30 %		
Rent & Occupancy			5 %		

(Continued)

Income Sources	This Request	Total Project Budget	% of Project Income	Total Agency Budget	Project % of Total Income
Utilities			3 %		
Insurance			1 %		
Marketing & Outreach			5 %		
Professional Development			4 %		
Mileage			5 %		
Equipment Rental/ Maintenance			2 %		
Project Evaluation			2 %		
Indirect or Overhead Cost			10 %		
TOTAL EXPENSES			100 %		

For a simple foundation proposal, it might look more like this table.

Categories	Expenditures	Revenues	
		From Grant	Other Sources
Salaries & Benefits	$ 1,880.00	$ 900.00	$ 980.00
Supplies	$ 500.00	$ 300.00	$ 200.00
Communication (phone, postage, web site)	$ 100.00	$ 50.00	$ 50.00
Mileage	$ 20.00	$ 0.00	$ 20.00
TOTAL BUDGET	$ 2,500.00	$ 1,250.00	$ 1,250.00

A budget for a government grant can be a several-page document, but the concepts are the same. The funder wants a graphic picture of where the money comes from and how it will be spent. In this chapter, you'll concentrate on how you want to spend the money in a series of worksheets to use as background for the budget you'll eventually submit. Don't worry if there are holes or if you have 16 messy versions. You'll rework the numbers a dozen times before you're finished.

Start with People

Personnel costs are usually the largest item in any project budget, whether the focus is microbiology research or outreach activities for gang prevention. Put on your list-making hat and start listing everyone who might possibly be involved in this project. Don't make final decisions about whether they are volunteers, paid staff, or outside consultants at this point. You can make some notes about how many hours per week you're apt to need their services and you can add their salaries, but the actual decisions about who gets paid from which grant, whose time is considered an organizational match and whose work is considered an in-kind donation can wait for awhile. Right now, the task is to create the ideal, top-of-the-line staffing pattern to ensure the success of your project.

If you need help in determining salary scales, ask someone in the agency's accounting or human resources department, call United Way for human service positions in your area, or search online for "nonprofit salary scales." If you go online, find a site like MySalary.com (http://swz.salary.com/salarywizard) that allows you to search by job title, zip code, and educational level for specific positions since national averages mean little and a home health case manager is different from a home health aide. Choose figures at the higher end of the range if special skills like being bilingual or knowing specialized computer programs are required.

The expense worksheet is a simple table I use as a budget starting point.

Expense Worksheet for _____ Project (1)

Personnel Title	Role in This Project	Annual or Hourly Pay Rate	No. of Positions	Hours or % of Time	Total FTE*	Estimated Cost

*Full-time equivalence: Because not all people paid under a grant will be working full-time or have 100 percent of their salaries covered by the grant, budget forms ask for FTEs or the percentage of time staff spend for each position. An FTE can range from miniscule for an executive director or senior research scientist in an advisory capacity (0.1 FTE or 10% which is 4 hrs/wk) to more than one for multiple people with the same job title (4.2 FTE for 7 child-care workers each working 30 hrs/wk).

Some positions to consider that are often included in project budget include:

- **Executive Director or Principal Investigator:** Unless you're a very small agency or this is a solo research grant, this person will not devote 100 percent of his or her time to the project. Budget forms often ask for "FTE" or full-time equivalents based on a 40-hour workweek. If the executive director or principal investigator has only peripheral management responsibilities for this project you might estimate his or her time at 4 hours/week or 0.1 FTE. In dollars and cents, if the person makes $80,000 annually, he or she would receive $8,000 from this grant. If this is a major focus for the organization, you can revise the figure upwards, but never go above 0.5 FTE for this position since funders expect these people to be management staff who are juggling many projects at once rather than concentrating on just one.

- **Program Director:** Depending on the size of the agency and the scope of the program, this person might be the primary staff member for the project (0.75 to 1.0 FTE) or play a supervisory role (0.1 to 0.25 FTE). Again, as a first step, simply list the annual salary and notes about the optimal percentage of time to be spent on different projects. If this is a new venture for the agency or if it involves extensive collaboration, the program director will spend considerable time working with community partners and the funding agency so estimate time needed for that.

- **Program Staff:** These are the people who will actually do the work: the research assistants and child-care workers, the lab technicians and the grief counselors, the tutors and the nurses. In this section, FTE takes on a slightly different meaning. For the adult literacy project we mentioned earlier, one full-time coordinator (1.0 FTE), six half-time instructors (6 people at 20 hours/week equals 3.0 FTE) and two child-care workers who work with the children while parents are in class (2 × 0.25 FTE = 0.5 FTE) may be appropriate and would equal a total of 4.5 FTE. For a research project involving periodic testing of human subjects in several parts of the world, scientists in each of four locations working 30 hours/week (4 people at 0.75 FTE = 3.0 FTE) might each have 4 student assistants working 10 hours/week (16 at .0.25 FTE = 4.0 FTE) for a total of 7 FTE for the project even though 20 individuals will receive funds from the grant. Again, we'll do the actual math separately for each proposal after we finalize the program narrative for that request. At this point, simply jot down some possibilities. From experience, I can assure you that you will revisit this section multiple times as you juggle program needs with available dollars. People are expensive, and caseloads are somewhat expandable and contractible.

- **Support Staff:** Like the executive and program director, these may be current staff who devote a limited time each week to this project or they may be people you will hire for this particular project. Be realistic. If the literacy program will involve many new people phoning for information and needing directions to classrooms, budget the receptionist's time accordingly. On the other hand, if there is considerable record-keeping, scheduling, and follow-up to do, but few drop-ins, the project may need full-time clerical support and the agency receptionist's involvement may be minimal. The same considerations apply in research projects.

- **Substitutes:** If your project requires consistent staff coverage and/or a fixed schedule like a residential treatment program, child development activities, education services, or emergency care, budget for substitute staff for key people. As an after-school child-care director, I drove the van and used volunteers as emergency staff members when other staff were sick, but I don't recommend it. Give yourself some protection by adding three or four days per month into the budget for people who need to be on the job for the program to operate.

Decide how to handle accounting, record-keeping, custodial services, and evaluation. Sometimes these tasks are simply folded into an existing staff member's responsibilities and a portion of that person's time is charged to the grant or counted as matching funds. Sometimes a data entry person, programmer, or bookkeeper is hired specifically for this project. Sometimes the evaluation is part of the program design and performed by program staff as part of their regular duties. Sometimes you may choose to hire an outside consultant as an evaluator or contract with a service to do payroll and other accounting functions. Follow the patterns of the organization where you work, and let the project dictate what makes the most sense.

Provide Benefits

When you have filled in the chart as completely as you can, it's time to add benefits. Once again, it's important to use information from your agency if possible so talk with someone in accounting or human resources. If you're writing for a small project in a small agency, your benefits may be limited to Social Security; which is required by law. If your host agency has more than 50 employees, you will need to provide health care insurance after 2012; if you're part of a larger agency, university, or medical center, you may have a cafeteria plan of benefits to deal with. Don't worry about who is eligible for which particular benefits, use a standard rate for everyone.

Expense Worksheet for _____ Project (2)

Personnel Title	Role in This Project	Annual or Hourly Pay Rate	No. of Positions	Hours or % of Time	FTE	Estimated Cost
						$
						$
						$
						$
						$
						$
				Total Staff Salaries		$
BENEFITS (_____ % of total salaries)						$
				TOTAL PERSONNEL COSTS		$

You will undoubtedly have discovered that this chart works best as an Excel spreadsheet so that when you add a forgotten person at the last minute or cut the bookkeeper's time from half- to quarter-time for budget reasons, the math does itself.

What About Specialized Consultants?

As mentioned earlier, you may not want to hire some people full-time. If they are already on the agency payroll, and you are just using a portion of their time, list them under personnel and deal with where their paycheck comes from internally. Also, don't call people consultants or contracted employees just because you don't want to pay benefits for them. The Internal Revenue Service (IRS) has definite rules over who can and cannot be considered an independent contractor and the fines are steep for both the individual and the employer if they are disregarded. The easiest way to protect yourself is to make sure all consultants you hire work independently rather than under your direct supervision, have other clients outside your agency, and are willing to itemize their services for you.

Expense Worksheet for _____ Project (3)

Personnel Title	Role in This Project	Annual or Hourly Pay Rate	No. of Positions	Hours or % of Time	FTE	Estimated Cost
						$
						$
						$
						$
						$
						$
				Total Staff Salaries		$
BENEFITS (_____ % of total salaries)						$
TOTAL PERSONNEL COSTS						$

Contracted Services/ Consultants	Role in This Project	Details		Hourly Rate	No. of Hours	Estimated Cost
						$
						$
						$
						$
TOTAL CONTRACTED SERVICES COSTS						$

Having said that, there are many tasks that are appropriately handled by independent contractors or consultants. Here are a few to consider.

- **Accounting:** A bookkeeper or payroll service may be sufficient, but if your focus is on your work, having the financial side of the grant administration in good hands is important.

- **Evaluation:** A simple project may be evaluated as the program progresses with staff collecting and recording data as they go along and the program coordinator or director analyzing and reporting the findings monthly or quarterly. On the other hand, if this is a pilot project for a major government grant or you want to show external validity for your findings, hiring an outside evaluator may be a wise move. Some government grants specify that evaluation must be handled by a consultant and tell you how much, or what percentage of your budget, can be spent on this item.

- **Training:** You may want to break this category down into several line items for your worksheet because there will be many opportunities for internal and external education. For board members, training might be involved if this is a capacity building project. Other possibilities could include staff orientation and ongoing in-service professional development, motivational speakers or "reward" for program participants, or a keynote speaker or workshop presenter for an agency-wide event. I'm sure you can think of other situations where some extra education would add to the quality and excitement of the project.

- **Specialized Skills:** Again, the list will vary depending on your situation. You may need a dietician to review child nutrition surveys and your meal or snack plan for your child-care program, a psychiatrist to supervise counseling interns, or a web designer to create your online presence. *One person with specialized skills you cannot include is the grant writer.* All federal agencies and most foundations specifically exclude grant preparation and fundraising activities from the grant. They assume that this is the responsibility of the agency seeking funds and belongs in the general operating budget. Do not try to hide this expense under a generic category or "miscellaneous." It's too much money and too easy to track during an audit. Furthermore, if you do pay a fund development person from funds for anything other than a capital campaign and you are discovered, you will be required to pay it back and the likelihood of receiving a grant from *any* other foundation or government agency will be next to zero. This also applies to executive directors of small agencies requesting grant funds for the time spent researching funding sources, meeting with program officers, preparing grant applications, and other activities we explore in this book. *Only work directly associated with the implementation of the proposed (and accepted) project can be paid with grant money.*

Operating Costs

With people in place to implement the project, you need to add space, utilities, computers, and supplies to help them do their job. Once again, as you continue filling in your table, make notes about how you arrived at each dollar amount. You won't put them in the actual budget you submit with your proposal but will use them in the accompanying narrative and need them for reference as you monitor spending during the program year.

Expense Worksheet for _____ Project (4)

Personnel Title	Role in This Project	Annual or Hourly Pay Rate	No. of Positions	Hours or % of Time	FTE	Estimated Cost
						$
						$
						$
				Total Staff Salaries		$
BENEFITS (_____ % of total salaries)						$
			TOTAL SALARIED PERSONNEL COSTS			$

Contracted Services/ Consultants	Role in This Project	Details		Hourly Rate	No. of Hours	Estimated Cost
						$
						$
			TOTAL CONTRACTED SERVICES COSTS			$

Operating Expenses		Details	Unit Cost	Quantity	Estimated Cost
					$
					$
					$
					$
					$
					$
					$
					$
					$
			TOTAL OPERATING EXPENSES		$

Once again, only operating expenses that have a direct use in the grant proposal can be added to the project budget, but you can cover some of your overhead costs if you use existing space, utilities, and equipment. The purchase of new equipment has its own category, but the maintenance and any charges for use of current phones, faxes, computers, copiers, etc., can be prorated in the budget for the grant. Here are common expenses to add to your budget form.

- **Facility Space:** If you are renting space and have some you can dedicate to the funded project, you can pay for that space out of grant monies. The same rule applies for any additional space you rent. If you own the building or are using space rent-free from a city or another agency, you can't charge for it, but you can use it as an in-kind donation or match later on in the budget.

- **Utilities:** Again, figure out what percentage of the electricity, gas, and local phone use the project staff will use. Installation of new phones, long-distance phone calls, and cell phones and their use by outreach workers should be kept separate and charged to the project budget. One word of caution: If everything in the office is jumbled together in one group working area and it would be difficult for a visitor to see boundaries, save facility and utility costs to include as part of overhead, which has a budget category of its own.

- **Consumable Supplies:** These include art, laboratory, craft materials, or other program supplies that will be used—and used up—by program participants or research experiments. Be careful about including food items. If you are holding cooking demonstrations for a food bank, or including cooking activities in life skills classes for adults with disabilities, it's okay to add food as consumable supplies. If, however, you are providing meals to children or seniors or supplementing staples donated to your food bank with fresh food, you need to apply for government funds allocated specifically for that purpose. And don't even think about adding a budget item for coffee and doughnuts for parent meetings or pizza parties for an end-of-the-year celebration. They will be disallowed before you can say "double cheese, please." The government still has a puritanical streak, and you'll need to find food for incentives and rewards from local resources.

- **Incentives:** Strangely enough after that last admonition, funds to honor clearly defined benchmarks reached by program participants and "stipends" or sample products for volunteers who participate in research trials are allowed by the government. Foundations still frown on such practices and would prefer you fund them internally. However, they do recognize the importance of volunteer recognition and will allow suitable items and events to be funded by grant money if volunteers play a major role in your project.

- **Supplies:** You know the rules now and are probably prorating these items in your head already. Include everyday supplies like paper clips, toner cartridges, and toilet paper in project overhead, consider them in-kind donations, or charge only for what you know will be used by the funded project staff. Postage and package delivery can be separated out however, as can printing and mailing house costs for marketing purposes.

- **Travel Expenses and Mileage:** The easiest and smartest way to calculate mileage is to check the current federal rates (www.gsa.gov) and use that for both airline and automobile reimbursement. With gas prices continually rising, I budget local mileage on the high side, especially if outreach workers or home visitors are involved in the project. I also encourage agencies to reimburse volunteers for mileage and add that to their grant budgets.

- **Workshops and Conferences:** Don't go overboard traveling to exotic places to attend conferences, but do expect to send appropriate people to at least one major professional conference and several regional workshops or mini-conferences. Both foundation and government funders expect you to keep abreast of your field and to network with colleagues, and they realize conferences are good ways of doing this. Some government grants require you to attend specific training sessions or meetings. Include travel, accommodations, registration fees, and per diem (food and incidentals) for each person for each event.

- **Contingencies:** This is just "grants-speak" for miscellaneous, and yes, it's okay to add a little bit for unanticipated expenses. Don't include this item if your total project budget is less than $10,000; and then limit your unexpected costs to less than 1 percent of direct expenses. A large contingency fund is an automatic red flag that tells funders you were in a hurry but wanted to get every penny they might give you, or you had a big expense like a grant writer you wanted to hide.

Paying for Equipment and Overhead

The rule of thumb is that anything that costs more than $500 and lasts more than two years is considered equipment and needs to be requested separately from supplies. You want to be careful when you add these items to government budgets, however, because technically all equipment bought by government dollars belongs to the government and not to you or your agency. I don't know of any agents in trench coats who have raided an office in the middle of the night to repossess a copier or 15-passenger van, but the auditor will want to see each item you purchased with a little sticker saying it is U.S. Property purchased under Grant #123987G. If you're a small human services agency, you can save yourself a lot of paperwork and hassle by buying equipment through a foundation or corporate grant or from private donations. Still, I've added a line in the revised table on the next page because research labs still find that's the path to follow for big-ticket items like scanning electron microscopes or hyperbaric chambers. Remember, however, the equipment stays with the institution and does not follow the person doing the research if that person moves to a new agency.

Expense Worksheet for _____ Project (5)

Personnel Title	Role in This Project	Annual or Hourly Pay Rate	No. of Positions	Hours or % of Time	FTE	Estimated Cost
						$
						$
						$
						$
						$
						$
				Total Staff Salaries		$
BENEFITS (_____ % of total salaries)						$
TOTAL SALARIED PERSONNEL COSTS						$

Contracted Services/ Consultants	Role in This Project	Details	Hourly Rate	No. of Hours	Estimated Cost
					$
					$
					$
					$
TOTAL CONTRACTED SERVICES COSTS					$

Operating Expenses	Details	Unit Cost	Quantity	Estimated Cost
				$
				$
				$
				$
				$
TOTAL OPERATING EXPENSES				$

Equipment	Details	Unit Cost	Quantity	Estimated Cost
				$
				$
TOTAL EQUIPMENT COSTS				$
TOTAL DIRECT EXPENSES				$
INDIRECT EXPENSES (_____ % indirect rate)				$
TOTAL PROJECT EXPENSES				

Indirect expenses (also called overhead) are the percentage of general agency operating expenses you can add to the budget without itemizing. These include salaries of administrative staff (including fund development and grant-writing staff), facilities and utilities if you didn't list them earlier, insurance, accounting fees, etc. If the institution you are associated with has a history of receiving government grants, check with a principal investigator to find the negotiated rate you are allowed to charge. If this is your first government grant, you will negotiate this rate when you establish your agency's credibility in Chapter 6. If you are applying to a foundation, they may specify the rate in their guidelines. It's often a percentage of the project budget or based on your total agency operating budget. If the foundation doesn't list an overhead limit, ask for 15 to 20 percent of basic agency costs.

Ask for What You Need, and Spend Everything You Receive

Before you total up your expense column, review the items a final time to make sure you didn't forget anything and that salaries and other costs are feasible. Funders expect you to spend every penny they give you on the project they approve. They also expect every line item expense to be within 10 percent of your budget projection. You may be able to negotiate a budget revision in mid-year, but that will be only within the approved funds for relatively small changes. If you underestimate what you need, that's too bad. You can't return to them for more money. If you have been extremely frugal and have some money left over, you'll have to give it back if it's government money. If you receive a grant from a foundation, you'll have an extremely difficult time explaining why you didn't spend it all in your final report—and you'll have an even more difficult time receiving funds for another project in the future.

Turning to Income

Except for some government agencies, most funders do not like to pay for your entire project and will ask you to specify other sources of funds both for the current year and for continuing the project without their support. While you can't comingle funds between accounts, you *can* ask more than one foundation to fund a particular project or to fund different elements of the same project. For example, a drug treatment program might receive state funds for basic treatment services and pay for art therapy, family reunification, and job training projects from foundation funds and community contributions.

Funders also want to know you are serious enough about your mission or research to pay for some of the expenses out of ongoing operating funds. Some grants require a specific ratio of matching funds in either cash or donated services and products. Income categories are fewer so it's easier to manipulate the columns to see who or where the funds will come from. This is shown in the sample income worksheet.

Income Worksheet for _____ Project

INCOME	This Request	Total Project Budget	% of Project Income	Total Agency Budget	% of Project to Total Income
Government Grants					
Foundation & Corporate Grants					
United Way					
Fundraising (Net)					
Individual Contributions					
Earned Income					
Interest Income					
In-Kind Support					
TOTAL INCOME					

Most of the categories are self-explanatory, but here is a brief description for each.

- "Fundraising" includes all money earned through special events such as candy sales, golf tournaments, tribute dinners, walk-a-thons, and the like, after the expenses for the event are subtracted.

- "Individual contributions" can be the result of direct mail, membership appeals, annual campaigns, and other gifts from small business firms and individuals.

- "Earned income" is the fees you charge for services. Studies have shown that people appreciate services more if they contribute at least a token amount. While you need to be sensitive to the economic situation of your program participants, it's wise to consider a sliding scale for activities such as workshops, concerts, youth activities, educational services, etc.

- "In-kind support" is anything that is donated. This can include staff and volunteer time, products to use in the delivery of services or in the office, expertise in reconciling the bank statements or fixing plumbing problems, items to use as attendance incentives, etc. The list is as long as your imagination and record-keeping expertise allows.

We'll return to the income part of the budget in Chapter 12 after we have a thoroughly refined program design and a specific funding source.

Budgeting for More Than One Year

Preparing the expense budget for two-, three-, or five-year funding follows the same process you have just used. You do *not* want to simply duplicate the Year One budget and pretend nothing will change, so you need to return to list making and brainstorming. Here are a few areas to explore.

- **Start-up Costs:** What supplies and equipment will you purchase the first year that will last the duration of the project? Will you need more desks, computers, and additional phones? Will you buy curriculum materials at the beginning of the project or will they need to be replaced each year? Will there be extra staff training required for a new program focus?

- **Personnel:** For some projects, the project director is hired first and other staff is added as activities are developed, so that personnel costs increase from month to month the first year and then remain steady the following years. In a capacity-building program, the grant may be used to fund a larger portion of a position like office manager or fund development director the first year, which decreases each year until the agency absorbs the cost in its regular operating budget. In another scenario, expenses for an external evaluator may be higher at the beginning and end of the project and minimal in the middle. Finally, cost of living increases and/or merit pay raises need to be factored into everyone's salaries.

- **Program Activities:** In some projects, the number of program participants stays the same over the duration of the program and the individuals receiving services change from year to year. In other situations, the numbers of people involved—and the expenses—increase from year to year. The budget for a theater program or an art exhibit will be different pre- and post-production. And if your research involves field work, costs vary by location, duration, and other factors specific to your program. You will have an opportunity to revise your budget each year, but once again, the funder expects you to know what you're doing and won't accept major changes.

- **Outreach and Dissemination:** Although these are vastly different activities, I've combined outreach and dissemination for budget purposes because they both use copious amounts of printing and promotional materials. You may purchase large banners and cable TV ads the first year to let the community know your museum is open for business and only continue with the ads—or change media to see if something works better the second year. You may publish videos or notebooks the third year as you train others to replicate your program—and you may need to advertise in professional journals rather than local newspapers. Establishing a database and email or mailing system for a concert series may cost more than maintaining it.

Once again, keep your worksheets so you can remember the changes you make. You will most likely be asked to submit an overview of your multiyear budget on a single page with separate columns for each year. This makes it very easy for review panels and foundation boards to see if their financial support follows your proposed activities. Because this is exactly what you want to demonstrate, make sure it does—and make sure you can answer any questions they may have about variations from year to year.

Moving On

After you identify potential sources of funds for your project in the next several chapters, you can return to the budget to clarify how you'll pay for the expenditures you've just created. When you get to completing the application forms, you'll turn the worksheets into much simpler charts to demonstrate where the money comes from and how it will be spent. At this point in the process, however, spend a few minutes congratulating yourself and celebrating the work you've already done to show you understand your fiduciary responsibilities.

ACTIVITIES

1. List the job titles for people you will need to implement your project. Estimate the percentage of time they will spend on the project and obtain salary ranges for comparable positions in your community.

2. Research the level of benefits your agency provides, and add it to your working expense budget.

3. List consultants who would add benefits to the implementation of your project and research prevailing hourly rates for each position.

4. Create a laundry list of operating expenses, including consumable materials and supplies.

5. Fill in a sample expense budget using the worksheet outlined in the chapter or a form your agency uses.

6. If you need equipment like computers, cell phones, microscopes, musical instruments, or specialized vehicles, research prices and begin the process for competitive bids if appropriate.

7. List potential sources of income and in-kind contributions you'd like to investigate.

chapter **4**

Proving the Need

> *Come, come, my conservative friend, wipe the dew off your spectacles and see the world moving.*
>
> Elizabeth Cady Stanton

People who review and make decisions about grants ask two basic questions:

- What difference will this research or program make?
- Are you the best person (agency) to do it?

The answers to these deceptively simple questions are sometimes difficult to state in words and even more difficult to demonstrate, but you must be able to do both before submitting a proposal for funding. In this chapter, we'll look at the need for the project (the difference it will make), and in the next chapter, we'll look at establishing your credibility as the best person or group to implement the project.

The first issue to clarify is whose need you're addressing. You may need a grant to meet payroll or replace the carpeting, but that's not the need the foundation or government is talking about. It's not even enough to say you have this intriguing scientific question that is begging to be answered. Your personal and agency needs and your scientific interests are your responsibility, and funders do not want to solve those problems for you. Grant makers want to know about the larger community need your project will address. Are you teaching adults to read so they can get a better job? Developing a new approach for treating the millions of people with arthritis? Stopping the destruction of the corn borer that has an impact on new sources of energy? What are you going to do that will make a difference in the world—and who will it benefit other than yourself?

Start with the Problem(s)

The best proof that a need exists can be found right in your own backyard. The first, and one of the most important, ways to identify need comes from your current participants and the people in your community. How long is the waiting list for child care for infants? What community issues repeatedly make newspaper headlines? What major employer opened or closed a division in your area? Include people who are intimately involved in your area of interest in your discussions as you make another list—this time of problems you want to solve with your proposed actions. Ask everyone you meet and listen carefully as you make the implicit characteristics of your problem as explicit as possible. At this point, most of the data will be hearsay information you overhear at the coffee shop, think you remember from an article in a journal, or surmise from listening and watching staff and clients interact. That's okay. You're looking for things everyone "knows," but no one says out loud. At this point, you are creating a rough list as the starting point for more formal research.

The table shows beginning lists that our three hypothetical grant seekers from Chapter 1 who want to serve illiterate adults, bring relief to arthritis sufferers, and stop the rampaging corn borer might construct.

Need for Proposed Project

Proposed Project	Teach Adults to Read	Develop New Treatment for Osteoarthritis	Stopping the Destruction of the Corn Borer
Identified Problems	High unemploy-ment rate	46,000 million people affected nationally	Loss of major cash crop for farmers
	People not hired because they lack reading skills	Determine the role inheritance plays in onset and severity of symptoms	Ripple effect of poor corn yield in other areas—fuel, animal feed, human consumption, adhesives, cosmetics, carpets, etc.
	People laid off because they can't read	Limited understand-ing of cause of pain	No accurate information on extent of problem

(Continued)

Proposed Project	Teach Adults to Read	Develop New Treatment for Osteoarthritis	Stopping the Destruction of the Corn Borer
	Can't help kids with homework so cycle repeats	Current therapies have major limitations	Existing pesticides are ineffective
	Embarrassment and feelings of failure	Conflicting information about effectiveness of different strategies	Few natural enemies found
	Few jobs available for unskilled workers	Different ideas about role of diet, exercise, and support groups in prevention and treatment	Generations of borer attack different parts of plant
	Current language classes focus on oral rather than written language	Questions about which patients will and will not benefit from surgery	Found in conjunction with other pests

As you may have discovered in making this list, all situations have two sides—and community problems often have elements of solutions in their midst. Let's continue our list making with some potential strengths and resources our three apocryphal grant seekers might know.

Resources Available to Deal with Identified Need

Proposed Project	Teach Adults to Read	Develop New Treatment for Osteoarthritis	Stopping the Destruction of the Corn Borer
	People have developed creative coping skills	Explore chiropractic, accupuncture, and holistic approaches	Selected hybrids seem to be resistant
	Some people are literate in languages other than English	Preliminary data on stem cell transplantation shows promise	Promising research at Iowa, Kansas, Penn State, and Nebraska Universities
	Adult Ed can pay for instructors	Connection between weight and osteoarthritis made	Changing harvesting methods seems effective
	First Baptist has space they'll donate	Cartilage cell replacement promising for some people	Changing crop rotation sequence seems effective

Illustrate the Perceived Need with Reputable Data

To demonstrate your need to someone outside your community, you'll need to construct a three-dimensional picture by using outside experts to validate your experiential knowledge and perceptions. It's not enough to say, "Everybody knows we need to do something about gang violence!" People who are willing to give large sums of money toward solving a problem are concerned with at least two more aspects: importance and impact.

- **Importance means the significance of the issue.** How vital is it to the health and well-being of your community? Who or what will suffer if nothing changes? What are the consequences if the problem is ignored?
- **Impact means the effect of your intervention.** Who will benefit from your project and how will they benefit? What will change? What differences will the larger community notice? What are the larger implications of your activities?

You can show your project has both of these qualities by using reputable data from a variety of sources. In addition to collecting demographic and statistical information to demonstrate the importance of the problem you are proposing to address, you will be researching and saving examples of model programs, best practices, and reports documenting research in the field to show the potential impact of your work.

Let's Get to Work

If you're proposing a research project, your first step is a thorough literature search of your proposed field of study. Go beyond what you normally do for an article you submit for journal publication. Trace the history of work in the field and be prepared to show how your project will add a new dimension, answer an unsolved dilemma, or refute a common assumption. Look at related fields to see what strategies, discoveries, and approaches you might have in common. Our entomologist wanting to stop the corn borer epidemic will want to go beyond consulting with agronomists, agricultural economists, and meteorologists to gather information outside academic walls from farmers, county extension agents, and major agricultural corporations like Cargill and Monsanto.

If you're proposing a community project, start with your current base of operation. Let's go back to the people you tapped for your list of problems and resources and codify some of that information.

- Research agency documents to show demand for your services and the changes needed in service delivery to meet changing needs.

- Conduct surveys of current program participants to determine desired expansion, changes, or additions to program offerings. Write your survey questions carefully to elicit thoughtful responses. Sometimes three-question, five-minute personal interviews are more effective than paper and pencil questionnaires.

- Meet potential clients as they come out of the post office, convenience store, church, Laundromat, or the WIC office and ask what they see as gaps in services in a particular geographic or program area.

- Compare notes with other agencies that may see the community from a different perspective.

Established Data Sources Add Credibility

You'll also need to collect information from sources outside your personal sphere. Because a literature search for community activities is a daunting undertaking, start with IssueLab (www.issuelab.org). This online organization archives research about social issues and shares it with a broader audience in the nonprofit sector. Contributions come from a variety of nonprofit organizations, foundations, and academic centers so it is relevant and reputable. When I checked in June 2010, they listed 504 contributing organizations and 4,454 available research works with more added each day. You can search the site by issue (aging, economic development, transportation, literacy, etc.) or geographic region and can register for free subscriptions to daily research updates and/or monthly e-newsletters.

For demographic information, start with the U. S. Census Bureau. The official census is conducted every 10 years, so the information in rapidly changing communities is almost out of date before the data is tabulated. Still, it's good baseline information and useful for showing trends over several decades. Fortunately, the Census Bureau recognizes its limitations and conducts interim studies, all of which are accessible at http://factfinder.census.gov.

- The **American Community Survey** (ACS) collects information such as age, race, income, commute time to work, home value, veteran status, and other data each year from approximately three million households nationwide.

- Population estimates are updated annually for areas with a population of 65,000 or more and every three years for areas with population over 20,000.

- An extensive economic survey is conducted every five years (years ending in 2 and 7) to measure a wide variety of activities in all industries including food services, manufacturing, arts and entertainment, and health and social services. Wholesale and retail establishments and both nonprofit and for-profit organizations are included. Reports are generated by metropolitan statistical areas, counties, zip codes, and industry.

If you get lost online and can't find what you need, phone the regional office of the Census Bureau and speak to a live person. Condense your request to as few words as possible ("I'm looking for information about grandparents raising grandchildren." Or "I'd like to know more about people who have used up their unemployment insurance.") to help the receptionist forward your call. You may be sent to several people, but once you connect with the right person, you'll have access to answers to questions you didn't know you needed to ask.

Closer to Home

Not surprisingly, however, some of the best proof of local needs can be gathered from local resources. Gatekeepers and frontline staff often spot trends before the rest of us do. It's helpful to talk with school secretaries to discover who is moving into and out of a neighborhood before deciding on the appropriate languages for the bilingual aides you add to the budget. Emergency room nurses are often the first to pick up on the newest illicit drugs in the community. Mom-and-pop markets will have added new products on their shelves and signs in their windows long before the census shows an ethnic shift in a neighborhood.

Obviously, the more people you know personally, the easier it will be to obtain information, so make an effort to attend public hearings about issues that relate to your project and introduce yourself to people who speak. This applies to both presenters and audience members since both may have information you can use. ("Hi, I'm Peter Piper, and I was interested in your comments about women and heart attacks. I'm working on a grant proposal to fund family exercise activities, so I wonder if we could talk more about this later.") Exchange cards or phone numbers, and write or call within a few days to set up an appointment to talk further.

If you need to make a cold call to an agency where you know no one, use the receptionist as your ally. Introduce yourself, briefly explain your purpose in visiting, and ask his or her advice about who you should speak with. ("Hi, I'm Peter Piper, and I'm working on a grant proposal to fund exercise activities for families to do together. I'm looking for information about city programs—or air quality—or more recent data than the census—or research on the benefits of exercise—and wonder who might be able to help me.")

Here are a few places to contact on a regular basis so they remember who you are. After several years, some of them will actually contact you when they have something they think you might be interested in knowing.

- **City Planning Department:** They often rely on census data but may have conducted a more recent study as part of a major planning effort or to support their own grant-seeking activities.

- **Police and Fire Departments:** If you make internal connections through networking, you'll have access to more recent data than what is published in the Uniform Crime Statistics by the FBI or from the state's attorney general's office. You can also get information on the extent and nature of gang activity, as well as informal assessments of neighborhood strengths and challenges that are difficult to find elsewhere.

- **Hospitals and Medical Centers:** All hospitals that accept Medicare reimbursement and other government funds must do a community health assessment once every five years. In addition to good information on local health issues, the studies often include other important demographic and community data. Because these assessments take considerable effort to produce, and few people ask for them, most hospitals are more than willing to share. I usually start my search by contacting the public information or the fund development officers because they tend to have an understanding of how I'll use the information—and they believe me when I say I'm not an investigative journalist looking for a scandal to report.

- **United Way:** Some United Ways conduct specialized community surveys whereas others maintain a database of relevant information on community needs for their member agencies. Most are very willing to share this information with anyone who asks.

- **Chamber of Commerce and Board of Realtors:** Ask to speak to the executive director or someone who has been in the community for a long time. When you meet this person, explain your project and how you are looking for information about the community that isn't written down. ("I'm working on a grant proposal to fund family exercise programs and I'm wondering about companies that have employee fitness programs—or might be interested in supporting such an effort—or offer exercise or wellness services to the public." Or "I'm working . . . and I'm interested in areas of the city where I'm most apt to find families with small children—or how people who live near parks use them—or how many homes in our area are apt to have exercise equipment in the basement or garage.") Most of the material you will glean from these sources will be anecdotal and informal, but you can discover historical facts that shed light on current controversies, learn about subtle shifts in neighborhoods that are not recorded on paper but can drastically affect program planning, and occasionally identify a valuable partner or funding resource.

- **New Fast Food and Other Franchises:** Before KFC or Payless Shoes or any other national company opens a store, they know there will be enough people matching their ideal demographics to make the venture profitable. The people that patronize their new store may have the same characteristics as people you want to serve in your project, so ask at franchises that are just opening in your area. The local owner/operator may not have the information, but he/she will be flattered you asked and will help you find the correct person at the corporate level. This calls for a personal visit during non-rush hours to explain your plans and how you'll use the data you're asking for, but if you take the time, you will have established a valuable ally for future requests including corporate grants and in-kind donations.

- **Newspapers:** I suggest local and regional papers online or in print take precedence over the more prestigious national ones simply because the information is more immediately relevant to establishing the need and importance of your project. When a car dealership razes a trailer park for expansion of its lot, the impact on the senior center, food bank, child care, and other programs in the neighborhood is felt immediately and drastically. When the board of education eliminates music in grade school classrooms because of budget cuts or a change in philosophy, a service gap is created to be filled by a community organization. When a university study is cited to illustrate changes in dietary habits, you can use both the feature story and the original source to support your request for adding an educational program to your food bank or weekly meal program. Copy and save the original article so you can return to it later. Depending on the context in which you eventually use the information, you may say, "According to the *Anytown Daily Journal*, obesity is a growing problem in the East Valley." On the other hand, you might want to do your own interview of the food bank director, quote a passage from the university study, or speak to the swing vote on the board of education.

- **Library:** With our reliance on the Internet, we often forget this valuable resource for reference help, for local information, for an environment where you can sift and organize material and ideas with few interruptions. Community and college libraries—as well as the nearest Foundation Center collection—are most welcoming places for grant seekers.

Traditional Sources of Statistics

Once you have gathered more than enough local data, check out federal, regional, county, and state agencies that publish reams of statistics online. The federal agencies listed in Chapter 9 have reports, white papers, and statistics that can be extremely valuable and are impressive sources to cite, especially if you are applying for a federal grant. Almost all information is now online, but if you plan to use a particular document extensively as reference material, you can obtain bound hard copies for a slight printing and mailing fee. Some sites are more user-friendly than others, and sometimes following a phone maze is necessary, but be persistent. The more recent and specific the data is, the greater your credibility is in the eyes of the funders—and the more useful the information is for program design and implementation. Some sites to explore include:

- **State Health Departments:** Enter the name of your state and "Health Department" into any search engine to find what the agency is called in your state. You may find several agencies (health, mental health, public health, health and human services, environmental health, etc.), and you may need to visit several sites to find what you need. Generally you can find state, county, and city health statistics for infant mortality, birth defects, cancer, hospitalizations, live births, mortality, age of mothers giving birth, medical care during pregnancy, sexually transmitted diseases, and similar information listed in state, county, city, and sometimes zip code tables. In California, several state departments contain links to CHIS

(California Health Interview Survey—www.askchis.com), which is an ongoing network of public agencies, private organizations, and individual researchers who share funds and findings to provide easily accessible data. Grant seekers can get quick statistics on topics under the broadest interpretation of health and wellness imaginable and researchers can apply to analyze confidential and/or geo-coded CHIS data for their own projects.

- **State Departments of Education:** Even if your project is not directly connected to education, information about your local school is a valuable indicator of what's happening in the community. All state departments of education maintain a database of proficiency test results, expenditures, specialized programs, and the number and characteristics of teachers and students by district and individual schools. Since the No Child Left Behind Act was passed in 2000, there are numerous indicators of student, teacher, school, and district performance. You can also find information about such things as student-teacher ratios, ethnic composition of both students and teachers, language diversity and proficiency, level of technology, the percentage of students receiving free and reduced-price meals, the number of children with disabilities and the kind of handicaps they have. You can even discover how many kindergarten children attend specific schools if you're unsure of where to locate your after-school child-care program. (Of course you can also phone the school district or the individual schools, but sometimes, an online source is easier on the weekend.)

- **The State's Attorney General's Office and the FBI:** If you're looking for crime statistics, both the state's attorney general's office and the FBI are the places to look. The National Incidence-Based Reporting System (NIBRS) that most local jurisdictions now use tabulates extensive data on 22 major crimes and arrest information on 11 others for cities with population over 100,000, states, and the nation. Since many statistics have been kept since 1929, this is good information for showing changes and trends. Be careful, however, because single years can be misleading.

- **2-1-1 Information and Referral Service:** This three-digit phone number was originally reserved by the federal government in 2000 as a human and social service directory to be used during disasters. Since then, it has grown to become a valuable everyday resource for individuals, police and fire departments, churches, and community agencies who want to access community social services. 2-1-1 is also a most valuable source of information for grant seekers because staff keep detailed logs of the number, geographic origin, and nature of all calls, and tabulate the information in frequent reports. Sponsoring organizations and the sophistication of the service varies from community to community, but enter a zip code, city, or state at www.211.org and find what's available in your area.

Making Generic Statistics Relevant

Now that you have computer files loaded with research reports and statistical information and a desk covered with printouts, it's time to figure out how to use it. *Data in isolation means nothing.* Your job as a grant writer is to choose the facts and figures that help you tell a story and demonstrate why you need the grant. Relying entirely on verifiable statistics will bore your reviewers to tears. Filling the pages with heart-wrenching stories of individual needs on the other hand will get you tossed in the reject pile just as quickly. You need to find the balance between objective information and emotional examples that tell the story of your project in ways that capture your readers' interest. In a similar vein, using only local data without placing it in a regional, state, and/or national context, and the flip side of using national or global statistics without tying them to local situations, is equally as ineffective.

Look at the material you've collected, and arrange it according to the grants you want to receive or the people you want to engage in the project. This will vary greatly depending on your field of interest and if you're working in an academic or community setting. For example, showing the unemployment rate of the zip codes you serve compared to county, state, and national levels can be a potent argument for your adult literacy project, as well as for job training, youth employment, economic literacy, affordable housing, food sufficiency, and a host of other social support services. How you present the data to the funder will depend on whether you are proposing a research study on factors contributing to unemployment, a thesis project looking at the implications of functional illiteracy in adults, or a direct service project teaching people to read.

On the other hand, if you find interesting statistics on the incidence of arthritis obtained from the national Centers for Disease Control and Prevention (CDC), you may use them to define and limit program participants for either research or community service projects even though the data is reported at national or state levels. For example, let's explore how you can make some reasonable assumptions about the number of potential participants in your area for the water aerobics part of your program design for people with arthritis. Since you know that 22 percent of the residents in California have been diagnosed with osteoarthritis and you have 50,000 people living within a 5-mile radius of your center, you can estimate 11,000 may be interested in your services. On the other hand, let's say 24 percent of the population is 65 or older and 58 percent of that population has arthritis in your state. Doing this math results in fewer than 7,000 potential clients. That's okay. Explain how you came to your conclusion, and you'll be fine. Both are reputable numbers, and you can figure out which you want to use depending on other factors in your proposal.

I often seek and sort information according to potential program participants. Using this method, our adult literacy grant seeker might collect material for three possible segments of the community: recovering addicts, Southeast Asian immigrants with children in grade school, and young adults who dropped out of school before getting a high school diploma. While some of the research might overlap, you can see immediately the diversity of the three populations calls for quite different documentation. For the proposal focusing on recovering addicts, you'll want statistics on the illiteracy rate among abusers who are incarcerated, as well as those who self-refer, and any correlations between illiteracy and recidivism would be helpful. Model projects that are combined with 12-step programs and reading materials with high-content/low-reading-level might also be valuable resources for this client population. Much of the same research might apply or be adapted for the young adults who have dropped out of school, although the emphasis will probably be more on lifetime earning ratios and a skills inventory for available jobs. Immigrant parents, on the other hand, will be attracted to the program if they see a direct connection between their learning to read and their children's success in school, and they may be more interested in books they can read as a family rather than books for their own pleasure or knowledge. If they are already literate in another language or if their culture places a higher value on oral rather than on written communication, supporting documents and program models will need to be decidedly different.

Condensing Your Data in a Case Statement

Your final task before turning to other steps in the process is to write the first draft of a need or case statement. *A need statement is a concise (no more than a page) description of the problem your program solves.*

- Choose the most compelling and dramatic examples.
- Focus on providing clear information about what must be changed and why it's important to change it now.

- Include available resources and community strengths to show progress toward solving the problem is possible.

- Show benefits to the program participants, the local community, and the larger society.

- Do *not* overstate your case. Less is better than more.

- Remember, your responsibility is to explain how the money will be used for a tangible project.

When you can clearly and concisely describe the problem you face and link it to more universal issues, you have taken a giant step in answering the first question raised at the beginning of the chapter. You will be able to say in two or three sentences *"This* is the difference my research will make!" or *"Our project is important because* _____*!"* Now it's time to turn to showing that you are the best person or agency to implement the project.

ACTIVITIES

1. List at least six community situations that describe the problem you want to solve.

2. Find three or more internal agency documents that show current participants need the service you want to provide or the research you want to do.

3. Ask seven or more current clients what benefits they would receive from the projected project.

4. Ask a dozen or more potential clients to describe the problem you want to solve in their own words.

5. If you are a member of a networking, service, or religious group, informally ask individuals for their perception of the problem you want to solve. If you are not a member of any such group, ask someone who is to invite you as a guest and ask your question casually as part of your introduction to new people.

6. Contact five or more local nonprofit, governmental, or civic agencies (or related academic departments) for relevant demographic or research information they are willing to share.

7. Identify and gather material from six or more county, state, or federal agencies.

8. Rework two or more national or generic statistics so they have local significance.

9. Connect two or more local findings to data from a broader sampling.

10. Write one sentence defining the importance of your proposal and one sentence describing the impact of your project in a single-page case statement.

chapter 5

Establishing Your Credibility

Clothes make the man. Naked people have little or no influence in society.

Mark Twain

In the last chapter, we established the importance of the *project*. In this chapter, we'll start to answer the second question funders ask: Why are *you* the most important person or agency to implement the program? To do this, we'll use the attachments and questions listed in foundation applications and government RFPs as guidelines. Many of them, like the IRS tax exemption letter and animal protection assurances, will simply be legal documents that prove you are a reputable organization that meets their eligibility requirements. Others, such as the agency history and your professional bio, may take some crafting. It's important to get an early start on collecting this material because some steps, including finding a fiscal sponsor or registering with the federal government, may take weeks or months to complete. Some will simply involve copying a form and obtaining a signature. You will need many of the documents for all the grant applications you submit, however, so it's a good idea to locate and store copies where they are easy to access. Fortunately, once you've amassed this collection of documents, you can simply pluck one sheet from each folder, make a few adjustments, obtain the appropriate signature, and have it ready for the next application.

Overview of Attachments

The following list is a compilation from several sources and is only meant for preparation purposes. Foundation guidelines and government RFPs will have a checklist of the specific attachments they want, and it's important to follow their instructions.

- Copy of IRS 501(c)(3) letter
- Roster of board of directors with related professional, community, and demographic information
- Organization chart showing decision-making structure and how proposed project is integrated into the larger agency
- Most recent audited financial statement
- Organization's current annual operating budget
- Projected operating budget for upcoming year
- Budget for proposed project
- Other funding sources for this request including amounts and whether received, committed, or projected
- Latest annual report
- Letters of support/commitment
- Compliance with government requirements
- Project-specific items like city permits, professional licenses, schedules of proposed activities, etc.
- Recent newsletter articles, newspaper clippings, evaluations or reviews
- Videos/cassettes (particularly if your request is for support of one of the performing arts)

Two actions take top priority if you have not already done so: securing the right to obtain foundation and/or government funds and registering with the federal government.

Although it is possible for individuals and newly formed organizations to obtain funding without a 501(c)(3) designation from the IRS, the chances are exceedingly slim. If, for example, you are a writer working on a novel or a botanist cataloguing native plants in a desert preserve, it's possible to find funders who will award you a grant or fellowship to do so. If you have a publisher or a letter of endorsement from the managers of the preserve, your chances for funding improve. If you are looking for a grant to travel outside the country to gather information, you will definitely want to partner with a writer or botanist in that country or a reputable global organization as a sign that you're serious about conducting research and not just taking a vacation. Similarly, if you want to teach writing to incarcerated women or conduct field trips for fifth-graders to your desert preserve, your funding search will be easier if you can show affiliation with a community center, religious organization, or other local agency. Funders want reassurance that their money will be well managed, and it's difficult for them to judge solo efforts. They are much more comfortable dealing with an organization that has gone to the trouble of incorporating and obtaining nonprofit tax status.

Choosing Between Incorporation and Fiscal Sponsorship

If you are already part of a nonprofit social service agency, hospital, medical center, college, university, research institute, or faith-based organization and will be conducting your project under their auspices, all you need to do is obtain copies of their 501(c)(3) tax-exempt designation letter from the IRS. You will need both the number (for blanks on the cover sheet) and a copy of the letter (as an attachment). Since you'll use these frequently, keep a dozen copies of the letter in an easily accessible file.

If you don't have a 501(c)(3) designation, you can either incorporate as a nonprofit agency on your own and apply for a charitable tax exemption or you can find an existing agency to act as a fiscal sponsor to accept and administer your grants. Gregory L. Colvin, a recognized expert in fiscal sponsorships, developed a useful comparison of legal factors between the two options for the San Francisco law firm of Adler & Colvin (www.fiscalsponsorship.com). He believes fiscal sponsorship is the best option for new, experimental projects wanting administrative and financial management. On the other hand, incorporating as a new 501(c)(3) makes better sense for projects with administrative and financial staff in place, a program with a track record, and a measure of assured funding. Incorporation takes time (from three months to a year), money ($1,000 to $10,000 or more in registration, legal, and accounting fees), and persistence. A fiscal sponsor is considerably cheaper (from free to 10 percent or more for management fees) and can accept grants and other contributions on your behalf immediately. There is no such thing as a free lunch, however, and fiscal sponsors and their board of directors ultimately have control over your project. Although in actual practice they usually delegate much authority back to an advisory committee and the project director, there will be a price to pay. This may range from minor annoyances like their wanting reflected prestige or obsequious acknowledgment to more meddlesome micromanagement of daily activities or attempts to adapt the project as their own. If maintaining autonomy and independence is important to you, incorporation is the way to ensure you retain control over your project. Of course, this isn't an either-or situation. Many small, new groups operate under a carefully selected fiscal sponsor for a year or two while they complete the incorporation process.

If you choose to incorporate, contact the attorney general in your state for the official requirements, application forms, and fees. These vary from state to state but usually come in prepared packets with technical support offered online, in regional workshops, and through phone consultations. If you need additional help, contact one of the Small Business Development Centers sponsored by the Small Business Administration (SBA) in conjunction with community colleges or SCORE (Senior Corps of Retired Executives), which are often found at Chambers of Commerce. Online directories of these two groups, which offer free services, can be found at www.sba.gov/aboutsba/sbaprograms/ sbdc/sbdclocator/SBDC_LOCATOR.html and www.score.org/findscore/ index.html, respectively. Ask specifically for someone who is familiar with nonprofit corporations when you call to make an appointment.

Now back to fiscal sponsorships. Basically, any nonprofit with a 501(c)(3) public charity designation can agree to an arrangement whereby they accept and manage grants and donated funds on your behalf. You will want to select an organization whose mission is similar to yours and who has a good reputation and solid financial base on its own. This might be an educational institution, the church or synagogue down the street, a professional organization, or one of the agencies you visited while you were developing your project idea and need statement. The Foundation Center has an excellent free tutorial dealing with individual grant seekers and fiscal sponsorships at http://foundationcenter.org/ getstarted/faqs/html/fiscal_agent.html. One resource they suggest that I found particularly helpful was the Fiscal Sponsor Directory (http://www.fisc.org), which lists 168 organizations in 31 states that have experience and are willing to serve as fiscal sponsors. You can search by state, service category, or keyword to find appropriate profiles, which include contact information, number of sponsored projects, fees, eligibility requirements, and types of services provided. The growth of new fiscal sponsors has accelerated exponentially since 2000 so this is worth investigating, especially if you are seeking funds for arts and culture (73 percent of the sponsors are willing to accept such projects.) or live in California (more than a third of the listings are located in the Golden State).

Registering with the Federal Government

If you have any intention of seeking a grant from a county, state, or federal government agency, you need to register either as an individual or as an organization by following the appropriate path at www.grants.gov/applicants/get_registered.jsp. If you are already incorporated or part of an educational, medical, or research institution, check first to see if your department or agency is already registered. If so, you may be able to skip to Step 3 of the process and request a username and password.

Registering is not difficult, but it will take from a week to a month or more to process so it's good to get it done early. The directions online are very straightforward and explain each of the five steps in the process in detail so I will only outline them here. Be warned, however, that the alphabet soup bubbles over from this point on. You may want to start a small glossary to remember what the acronyms mean since they are not always explained in other government documents. (Many are listed in the Glossary at the back of this book.)

1. **Obtain a DUNS number:** The federal government uses the Data Universal Number System (DUNS) to identify your organization. You'll be directed to http://fedgov.dnb.com/webform/displayHomePage.do, where you will get your number almost immediately.

2. **Register with CCR:** The Central Contractor Registration (CCR) sets up your user account (E-Biz POC or E-Business Point of Contact) and identifies which staff member(s) are allowed to submit applications electronically. These people then become AORs (Authorized Organizational Representatives). Although you need to renew this registration yearly, it's wise to register only people who have authority and longevity within the organization for continuity purposes. You will be asked for an Employment Identification Number (EIN) or Taxpayer Identification Number (TIN). If you have one, this part of the process will continue and your E-Biz POC will be ready in about a week. If you don't have an EIN or TIN, you'll need to get one from the IRS, which adds another week or two to the process. Don't despair. These registration numbers will be used repeatedly for many foundations, as well as government grants, so they are worth the time and effort it takes to get them.

3. **Create Username and Password**: After you register with the CCR, AORs must wait one business day before they complete a profile and choose a username and password (M-PIN). These will serve as the electronic

signature when submitting an online application and should be guarded with your life. The speed of this step depends on how quickly the AORs complete their profiles, but theoretically it can happen in one day.

4. **Authorization:** Here's where you may need your glossary, but I want to give you a taste of bureaucratic language so here is an abbreviated summary of the government's explanation of this step. "When an AOR registers with Grants.gov the organization's E-Biz POC will receive an email notification . . . The E-Biz POC must then login to Grants.gov (using the organization's DUNS number for the username and the 'M-PIN' password obtained in Step 3) and approve the AOR . . . When an E-Biz POC approves an AOR, Grants.gov will send the AOR a confirmation email." Okay, to translate, it's just like getting a confirmation of a book you ordered from Amazon.com—half a dozen emails will arrive telling you that you just did what you did.

5. **Tracking AOR Status:** If you become impatient waiting for the collection of information from Step 4, there is a process to see if you've been approved or not as an AOR. I'm not sure there is anything you can do about it if you're not approved, but knowing they haven't forgotten you can sometimes be reassuring.

Updating GuideStar File

For years, grant seekers have used GuideStar (www.guidestar.org) to research foundations through their IRS returns. By looking at total assets, income received during the year and program-related investments, interested parties were able to make predictions about future funding trends for particular foundations. The files also include information about officers, directors, trustees, employees, and contractors, as well as grants and contributions made during the previous year, which gives you a head start on deciding if this is a viable foundation for your project. GuideStar is still an excellent source for basic information about family foundations and small foundations that do not maintain sophisticated web sites. In the last decade, however, the table has been somewhat turned and foundations are increasingly using GuideStar to do research regarding agencies that apply for grants. If your agency files an annual IRS 990 form, you are already listed in GuideStar—or rather, the information you provide the IRS is listed. Since this probably does not convey the complete picture you'd like to present to the public, GuideStar gives you the opportunity to upgrade the information. It's free, it's easy to do, and it establishes instant credibility with funders who can easily match what you report to the government with what you write in your proposal. Because there is space for funding and volunteer needs, GuideStar can also serve as a reference for potential donors.

Gathering Basic Agency/Individual Information

Now that we have some of the legal paperwork started, let's look at the information you need to gather about your agency or, if you're applying as an individual, about yourself. First, collect what you already use to describe yourself and your work—agency brochures, résumés, mission statements, previous grants, press releases, elevator speeches you use to introduce yourself in 10 seconds— anything and everything you have that says, "This is who we are and what we do." These are good places to begin because we will adapt them for each proposal. Now look at each piece from the perspective of your proposed project.

- **Mission Statement:** Summarize the mission of the agency or your individual career goals in two or three sentences. Reduce that to one sentence or one phrase. Keep all of your notes because eventually you will mix and match words to fit your mission to the mission of the funding agency.

For example, a music academy's mission statement in its entirety could be:

- *To enrich the lives of individuals and the community through music*
- *To provide outstanding instruction for amateur and aspiring professional musicians of all ages*
- *To reach out to the community through diverse programs and public performances*
- *To promote and nurture a lifelong passion for music*
- *Most importantly, to make music education available to all . . . one note at a time*

Each of these phrases might be used alone for a different funding source. The first phrase could accompany a request for a series of community concerts. The second would fit either training for instructors or scholarship funds. I might combine elements of the first and third phrases into something like "to enrich the lives of individuals and the community through diverse musical programs and public performances" in proposals for a jazz summer camp, concerts at elementary schools, student recitals at retirement communities, or the creation of a mariachi band or African drumming group. The final phrase might even find its way into an appeal for a customized software and data entry staff person to computerize student, alumni, and donor records.

- **History:** Condense 50 years or expand 3 years into a single paragraph that explains how you started and how far you've come. Our music academy could write: *Four music teachers responded to budget cuts in public school music education by creating a community school of music in a church basement in 1970. During the first year, they struggled to keep music alive for 43 young people from 31 families with volunteers providing individual and group lessons with a poorly tuned piano. Today, approximately 600 students between the ages of 6 months and 83 years choose from a wide variety of instruction and performance opportunities facilitated by a staff of 30 professional voice, percussion, woodwind, and brass musicians operating from two classrooms, 18 teaching studios, a keyboard lab, and an 80-seat recital hall.*

- **Specific Research or Program Activities in the Past Five Years:** What concrete success stories can you tell? Collect both quantitative and qualitative examples that show your work is important and makes an impact. Gather information that demonstrates the ripple effect of your work. To continue with our example, the music academy could outline the introduction and growth of two or three major activities and list the accomplishments of several alumni.

- **Current Research or Program Activities:** This variation of the previous section allows you to provide more details about one program, describe the progress of a "typical" student, and show how the proposed project will strengthen your current work. Use concrete specific examples to show how what you are doing now relates to both the past and the new direction you want to take. Will the grant help you extend current work to a new population? Add new elements? Explore a new direction?

- **Major Sources of Funds:** Know where you get your money now. Find a copy of this year's total agency operating budget. In addition, create a list of all grants and large donations from the past five years. Finally, you will need copies of the latest audited financial report for the agency to enclose as an attachment. If you don't have an audited report, you can ask if a review by an outside source will suffice. Often, if the grant request is small and the agency is new, reviews will be accepted.

- **Professional and Community Organizations and Awards:** List them all in one place so you have everything spelled correctly and don't forget any.

You can choose which to use for which proposal just like you do with listing community organizations on your personal résumé. The music academy will want to mention membership in the National Guild of Community Schools of the Arts and the National Federation of Music Clubs in all of its applications. If the funder places a high value on local community involvement, they might want to add their participation in three Chambers of Commerce and the award they received from a mayor for contributions to city life.

At this point collect everything. Make notes. Play with the words. Add things as you think of them. You will be condensing this material to one or two paragraphs in the proposal, but you want to be sure you remember the important details.

Describing Your Community and Constituency

If you condensed the information on community needs and resources you collected in the last chapter into a few paragraphs, you can almost skip this section. Notice I said "almost." There is still work to be done in deciding how to present the information to an outside audience that doesn't know all of the neighborhoods in Detroit or Atlanta and doesn't distinguish between the umpteen forms of cancer with different research efforts and treatment protocols. Your job is to bring the proposal reader/reviewer directly into your world so they can see, hear, taste, smell, and touch the environment you experience every day. Dry statistics will not do this so you will need to collect and use sensory adjectives, action verbs, and telling details. Let's look at how to describe your community and your constituency separately.

Community Profile

- **Describe the geographic area you serve.** Do you limit your work to one city? One neighborhood? Is your scope regional or national? I grew up in eastern South Dakota and learned in grade school to say, "We live 20 miles from the Minnesota border and 325 miles from the Black Hills." I also learned to describe my father's work as "studying seeds and soils" instead of "agronomy." You need to picture where you are in relation to someplace the person reading your proposal may have visited. If your field is in the sciences, you need to make the most sophisticated microbiological or psychological research project understandable to someone with the proverbial seventh-grade education.

- **Give a brief history of the area.** Were marshes reclaimed for housing for the Air Force base established in WWII? Did the city grow (or decline) as a result of being a "company town"? Is it a traditional home for new immigrants? What ethnic groups have called it home? What was the effect of a new highway, the introduction of big-box stores, or a major fire on the residents? In research, the questions will be different but similar as you trace the highlights of work done by previous scientists and show the effects of new technology on your field.

- **Tell a little about your relationship with other organizations in both the geographic and service/research arenas.** This may be a duplication of the groups you have already collected, but you can extend it to include competitors and partners. For example, the music academy might say: *"We are the only classical musical academy within a 25-mile radius of Evergreen College. Six music stores in the area offer play-by-ear lessons on electronic keyboards and three dance/music studios focus on popular vocal and dance performance."* If you are a branch of a national health, youth, religious, or other organization, you will want to mention that and describe your relationship with the larger body.

- **Show how the location affects your proposed project.** This will be implicit in some of your earlier statements, but it's important to make it explicit. Someone conducting research on air quality and asthma in conjunction with researchers from several institutions will want to include the locations of the sites to show similarities or differences of environmental conditions as well as mentioning the prestigious nature of the partners to demonstrate scientific rigor and note opposing theories and methodologies.

Constituency Profile

- **First gather information on current and past participants in your agency's programs.** Start with the number of unduplicated participants and look at as much information as you can find for as many years as records have been kept. This includes standard demographics like age, gender, language, ethnicity, city of residence, and income level, but it should also include characteristics that are specific to your project. You may want to note the average length of time in program, number of people with disabilities and the type of conditions, sexual orientation, medical history, etc.

- **You will also want to define the characteristics of people you will recruit for the proposed project.** How will they be different from and similar to current participants? Will the traits of your clients match the larger community demographics or will you serve a specific segment? Either is okay, but you will need to explain the rationale for your choice. While you can't exclude people from participating in agency activities on the basis of race, class, gender, sexual orientation, disability, or religious preference, not all programs are appropriate for all people. Most federally funded programs have income and age requirements for eligibility and you can add additional criteria for enrollment in your project. You can also add priority criteria that make programmatic sense such as giving preference to siblings in a family, children from single-parent families, teen parents, adults who have had a stroke or debilitating fall, etc. Be specific about the demographics of your intended program participants, how those characteristics mirror or differ from community data, and the reason these attributes were chosen.

- **Include information from alumni success rates.** Collect evaluation data from agency self-assessments and/or previous grants. In a senior wellness program, you may want to collect anecdotal information or support letters about improved quality of life. In substance abuse recovery programs, you need some data on how many "graduates" are still clean and sober, even though definitive statistics may be impossible to gather. In clinical trials, this translates as evidence of your track record or results of preliminary experiments.

- **Finally, don't forget your volunteers.** In many social service agencies, volunteers play a major role in many community organizations so be sure to describe both their demographics and their contributions.

Defining Your Organizational Structure

Funders are interested in learning how your organization works so they can predict how well the grant will be administered. While the application may or may not request narrative information about board and staff roles and responsibilities, a traditional organization chart is a universal requirement. Like so many other things in a grant proposal, this needs to be customized for each application. Yes, you can start with a boilerplate edition, but you need to change it to show how this particular project will fit into the agency's ongoing operations or how partners will interact in a collaborative effort. You will develop a similar diagram when you have decided whether or not you will have partners. For the time being, let's focus on internal operations as they are now.

You can add or subtract boxes to the generic one below to fit your situation, but these are the elements I think are important to include.

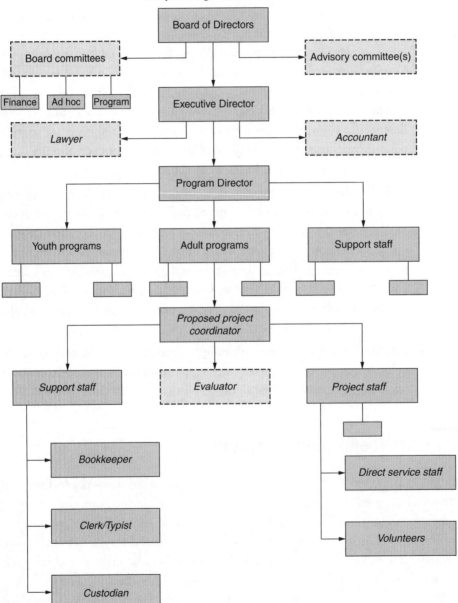

Nonprofit organization chart

Let me add a few notes to explain why I listed some items, left blank boxes, and made other changes in a typical business organization chart.

- A list of board committees shows both fiscal and programmatic knowledge and responsibility on the part of the board.

- Most government grants require an advisory council or committee, in addition to a board of directors. While these usually do not have policy-making responsibilities, they provide valuable technical and community input for program development and monitoring.

- The executive director or chief operating officer is the person with ultimate authority for day-to-day operations of the agency. In an all-volunteer organization, this role may be filled by the president or by an experienced volunteer.

- To keep things relatively simple, I've chosen to list some professional staff as outside consultants and categorized in-house employees simply as program or support staff. In addition to the accountant and lawyer I've specified, your agency might also outsource fundraising, custodial, and payroll duties. On the other hand, these responsibilities plus web site maintenance, community relations, marketing, and human resources might be internal positions or departments. I tend to list specific job titles if they are related to the proposed project and leave other boxes blank. I also make no distinction between paid and volunteer positions except for adding a simple asterisk to volunteer jobs.

- Because you want to show where the new project will fit into the existing structure, the final branch of the organization chart will be more detailed. Again, I've been generic in my chart so you can add your specific jobs, but it's important to spell out every position that you list in your project budget. Be sure to also include volunteers since you will mention them in your narrative, estimate their monetary equivalence as in-kind donations, and probably won't be able to survive without them.

Focusing on the Chain of Command

Because all proposals need to be approved by a board of directors, college administration, or other governing body before they are submitted, it's important for you to learn how the governance system and chain of command operate in your agency. Most importantly is who wants and needs to be involved in the development of funding proposals. In order to allow enough time to deal with feedback, secure necessary approvals, and meet your deadlines, it's important to discover (or establish) these expectations before you consider writing your first proposal.

A common process is to provide the board with a yearly listing of grants for which the agency intends to apply with quarterly updates on additional grant opportunities and the status of applications and awards. Once contracts have been signed, you will also want to regularly report on implementation activities, but that comes later. Some boards may want less involvement in the process so they may delegate funding oversight and program monitoring to subcommittees who make periodic reports in writing to the entire board. In this instance, the board president may want an individual briefing before signing the required documents. Other boards, particularly those in new or small agencies, may want more involvement in the development and actual production of the grant submissions. Depending on the system, you may need to return to the governing body and other administrators several times with a concept paper, first draft, and one or more editions of the narrative and/or budget.

Addressing other questions in the application about the board of directors is easy after you have figured out how they make funding and program decisions. Common subjects you may be asked to address are:

- **Board Roster:** As a minimum, funders ask for a list of board officers and members and their professional affiliations. If some of the members are retired, list them as "former superintendent" or "retired business owner" or a similar title. In addition to professional backgrounds, add community affiliations such as membership on other boards, appointed or elected position, or notable community recognition. Some foundations ask for demographic information. Even if they don't, you might include a sentence or two describing the diversity of skills, experience, ethnicity, or age that adds to the board's effectiveness.

- **Board Structure:** How long do members serve on the board? Are they elected or appointed? How are officers selected? How often does the board meet? Do they operate as a whole or through committees? What are the standing officers and committees?

- **Decision-Making Process:** Does the agency have a strategic plan with long- and short-range goals? Do they conduct a yearly agency self-assessment? Do they participate in ongoing board development activities?

- **Board Commitment:** To assess whether the board is an integral part of the organization or simply a figurehead, funders often ask the percentage of board members who made financial donations to your cause during the current fiscal year. If the dollar amount is impressive, you can make note of that in the narrative, but the important number is the percentage of board donors. If that number is less than 100 percent, this is the time for the executive director or board president to contact the stragglers. Grassroots organizations and those with low-income representatives on the board often balk at this expectation, but it is a crucial one. Funders wonder why they should give money to an agency when the people who presumably have the most investment in its survival don't contribute. The dollar amount doesn't matter, but the percentage does!

- **Advisory Council:** Is there a current advisory group in place to meet other funding requirements, offer specialized advice or skills, or serve as a fundraising arm of the agency? If there is and its existence is relevant to the proposed project, include the group in the narrative and organization chart and describe what will happen if the requested grant also requires an advisory council.

Gathering Support Letters

An important dimension of showing your competency in implementing the proposed program is to collect and submit good letters of support from past and potential collaborators. A collection of well-written support letters is a potent means of documenting the extent and depth of your collaboration with others by showing your history of working together, your mutual respect and reliance on each other, and the unique resources and skills each agency brings to the project.

The operative phrase in the above paragraph is "good letters." A collection of form letters simply copied on different letterheads will do more harm than good to your cause. What you want are sincere, credible views on the problem you've identified and reinforcement that you are the best or right person or agency to implement the proposed solution.

Agency executives are busy people and writing a support letter from scratch is often relegated to the bottom of the to-do pile. Here are some suggestions for ways to ensure you have the quality letters you need and deserve.

- **Include potential letter writers in the proposal process.** Community meetings or an interdisciplinary brainstorming session are excellent ways to hone the needs statement, discover hidden resources—and identify individuals and agencies to ask for support letters. Mention projects you're considering at networking and professional meetings and ask for people's input and their willingness to write a letter of support at a later date. Ask people in related fields for their sources of information on demographics, research, successful programs, etc. You don't need to use everything you collect, but asking for help is an easy way to gain program support.

- **Ask early.** Your chances of receiving a thoughtful letter are exponentially increased by the amount of time you give the writer. Of course, many of us are procrastinators par excellence, but if you give me three weeks to create a letter, the two-and-a-half weeks I think about it will show in the richness of the words, tone, and examples I eventually use. I may need a gentle reminder that the deadline is approaching, but both the content and flow will show I've been considering your request. On the other hand, if you call on Monday because you need a letter by Wednesday, you'll get a slightly re-warmed version of what I wrote for the counseling center down the street.

- **Ask the relevant person.** The executive director of a collaborating agency or the principal investigator in a similar research project are often the appropriate people but don't overlook a program director who is intimately involved with the population you want to serve or the precinct captain in the geographic area where you propose to build your transitional living home for first-time offenders. The content of the letter matters more than the title following the signature, so choose the person who knows the most details about your agency and the proposed program.

- **Ask personally.** You've given people warning in a meeting or another conversation, but you also need to officially request a letter either in writing or through a one-on-one phone call. No one thinks you're talking to them when you make a statement like, "You know, I'll need everybody to write me a support letter for this grant proposal I'm writing."

- **Provide specific information about the content and comments you want.** To avoid form letters, give people an outline or a sample letter with lots of holes. Start with the specific name and address of the recipient of the letter. "To whom it may concern" doesn't place either you or your supporter in a good light. Include information about your proposed activities. Ask the writer to describe basic information about themselves and their work, how they know you and your agency, and how you will work together on this project. Include individuals as well as organizations. You can decide which ones you want to use later. A sample outline for a principal whose campus has been selected as a site for a music education program could look something like this:

> *Thank you for agreeing to write a support letter to the MacAdams Foundation in support of The Mozart School of Music's request for funds to hold Instrument Petting Zoos at Washington Elementary School.*
>
> *I would appreciate receiving the letter on school letterhead on or before February 5, 2011, for our February 10th deadline.*
>
> *Please address the letter to: Ms. Adrian McAffey, Executive Secretary*
> *MacAdams Foundation*
> *9876 Cataract Circle*
> *Aurora, AZ 62339*
>
> *In the body of the letter, I'd appreciate the following information:*
> - *Description of Washington's student body and their knowledge of musical instruments, the current music program, its importance, and the effects of anticipated budget cuts on music education;*
> - *Brief history of other projects that Washington and Mozart have done together; and*
> - *Overview of our respective roles in the Instrument Petting Zoo project and what you hope your students will gain from the experience.*
>
> *Thank you, in advance, for your support. It's always a pleasure working with you and your staff. If you have any questions, don't hesitate to call me.*

On the other hand, a sample letter for a colleague who agreed to support a research project might look something like:

February 5, 2015

Dr. Dorian T. Sandeson
SRB Fund
One Corporate Way
San Pedro, TX 345656

Dear Dr. Sandeson,

I am pleased to offer my support to Priscilla Bowen in her research efforts on tracking insulin granules within pancreatic beta cells at the Scopes Laboratory of Unknown University.

I know Ms. Bowen through _____.

Her work is similar/different from/complementary to my research into _____ and will provide _____ to the field of _____.

I expect _____ will be an additional outcome of benefit to _____.

Because of my interest in Ms. Bowen's work, I am prepared to _____ for this project (at no cost to the SRB Fund) (as consultant funded by the SRB Fund).

With support from the SRB Fund, I look forward to _____.

Sincerely,

- **Send a gentle reminder.** If you haven't received a letter a week before your internal deadline, a simple email or message on their voice mail is enough to jog their memory. Take a light tone. If you receive no response within two days, speak to the person personally and see what you can do to help. If this is a crucial letter, offer a first draft for their revision and signature. Reassure them that you'll reciprocate with a letter for them when they need one. If time is running short, offer to have someone pick it up.

- **Choose the strongest letters.** You don't have to use every support letter you receive. Follow the funder's guidelines—some have restrictions on the number they'll accept—but narrow your choices to only those that add a dimension to your proposal. Keep the others in the file to use for backup and for testimonials in future publicity.

- **Thank everyone.** This includes people who wrote letters you didn't use. Thank them repeatedly—in a brief note the week after the proposal is submitted, the next time you see them, and when the contract arrives. Thank you is easy to say, and this will make it easier to receive another good letter the next time you ask.

Collecting Other Materials

When I started writing grant proposals in the early 1970s, application packets would grow to 60 to 70 pages by the time we finished adding attachments. Now the trend is to drastically limit what is submitted. Some foundations and even a few government agencies, however, still ask for materials attached to the application form or narrative. If you're asking for child development funds, for example, you will probably be asked for a diagram of the classroom and playground, the daily schedule, and a week's lesson plan with menus. Requests for research dollars frequently need to include summaries of preliminary data or abstracts of published articles. A youth symphony might enclose a CD or video of their last performance, whereas an art museum might add the program for a recent exhibit. Newspaper clippings and magazine articles can occasionally be relevant to dramatically depict a situation in a particular neighborhood if the project involves community organizing or to underline the eminence of a partner or proposed resource person, but use them sparingly. If your narrative doesn't convince funders of the need for your project or they don't recognize the name of the partner or expert, chances are a reporter's words won't make a difference. A letter from a child receiving school clothes and a backpack is much more effective than a newspaper article stating you held a back-to-school event at a local store. Newspaper clippings, agency brochures, programs from events, and other peripheral information are most useful for remembering details and borrowing phrases when it's time to write the narrative so gather and keep them in a safe place whenever you find them. Don't include them in the proposal unless you are specifically asked to do so.

Completing Government Requirements

The final step in collecting materials to show the credibility and competency of your agency is to identify and separate the assurance required by the government. Every government RFP package comes filled with documents to sign to show you understand and will comply with county, state, or federal regulations. Depending on the nature of the grant request, some corporate and private foundations include the same documents. Many will be familiar, like the non-discrimination or treatment of human or animal subject assurances. Others may be new to you. If you have any questions, read the fine print carefully and consult with your legal advisor because some may have fiscal or programmatic implications you need to know about. Because these documents *must* be signed and included with your application if you want to receive a government grant, group them together for the appropriate person's signature when the proposal is ready for signing.

ACTIVITIES

1. Locate the 501(c)(3) tax exemption letter or find a fiscal sponsor.
2. Write three variations of your purpose or mission statement to match three imaginary funders.
3. Describe the history of your agency or research in one page. In one paragraph.
4. Describe your current programs or research activities in one page. In one paragraph.
5. Profile your geographic or research community and show how it impacts your project.
6. Profile your intended program participants.
7. Describe your chain of command or governing structure.
8. Sketch an organization chart showing how your project fits into the larger organization.
9. Write a sample support letter for an imaginary agency to adapt on your behalf.

chapter **6**

Considering Ethical Issues

The most important persuasion tool you have in your entire arsenal is integrity.

Zig Ziglar

An important aspect of your professional or institutional credibility and reputation is the manner in which you handle ethical issues. Because we deal with people, money, products, and services, we deal with ethical situations in every grant proposal we write. Some of the concerns are in the public spotlight, like stem cell research or how we treat animal and human subjects. Others are more subtle and private, such as the quality of donated blankets we choose for distribution in a homeless shelter or the decision about accepting funds from a soft drink manufacturer to offer nutrition education in a classroom. Almost one-fourth (24 percent) of the people who responded to an AFP Quick Poll conducted by the Association of Fundraising Professionals in the July 6th issue of AFP eWire said they found themselves confronted with an ethical situation, challenge, or dilemma about once a month in their fundraising activities. Five percent (5 percent) faced an ethical situation two or three times a week. While those of us who concentrate on writing grant proposals may deal with ethical issues less frequently, I suggest we follow the advice of Peter Singer, professor of bioethics at Princeton, when he invites students to *think about ethical decisions more explicitly, to reflect on our intuitions, to be open about the fact that many things are moral issues, and to consciously think about what we ought to do.* Examining moral decisions is woven throughout *Grant Writing Demystified*, but the subject is so important it deserves a chapter of its own.

In 1964, the AFP developed 25 standards for its 30,000 members to review and sign annually in a Code of Ethical Principles and Standards. While they are designed for individuals and companies who raise funds in a variety of ways for agencies as a profession, the topics are relevant and need only slight interpretations for those writing their first proposals for grants for more personal causes. To read the complete copy with examples of both ethical and unethical behavior, which were amended in 2007, see www.afpnet.org/files/Content/Documents/CodeofethicsLong.pdf. I've chosen a few standards to highlight as most applicable to the scope of this book.

Doing No Harm

Like the Hippocratic Oath medical professionals take, our first responsibility is to refrain from any activities that harm the people and institutions we work with. The first AFP Standard is clear: *Members shall not engage in activities that harm the members' organization, clients, or professions.* This may seem obvious, but many actions have unintended consequences and the line between accepted practices and innovative program design is easily blurred. Think of the people whose well-meaning actions were perceived as kidnapping children after the Haitian earthquake, or the introduction of infant formulas to third-world countries that resulted in malnutrition and infant deaths when products were diluted with polluted water. Pain studies in mice, larger animals, and humans open valuable doors to future management of physical suffering but raise questions about the severity of the stimuli administered and the welfare of the subjects. When do the ends justify the means in offering language and other assimilation and acculturation programs for immigrants? Each field has its own areas in which physical, emotional, cultural, and other broadly defined "harm" can occur. It's important to identify these areas and define ethical boundaries for ourselves before we begin to look for money to fund a project, so keep your eyes and ears open for panel discussions of ethics in professional journals and at conferences. When you see a media exposé of the latest medical or social scandal, ask yourself what you would do to prevent or respond to such a situation. When you have a question about boundaries, ask someone with more experience, or someone you know has a skeptical view of your work. As science fiction writer and journalist Jerry Pournelle says, "In any ethical situation, the thing you want least to do is probably the right action."

One resource that is particularly helpful in the scientific community is the Principal Investigators Association (www.principalinvestiators.org). You don't have to be a member or the lead scientist on a research project to take advantage of their free weekly eAlerts that deal with research, administration and financial issues. Because the PI eAlert covers a wide range of non-science duties and responsibilities, including time management, team building, and ethical questions, I always scan it even though I never set foot inside a laboratory. If you're directly involved in research, their companion Lab Animal eAlert and Clincal Trial eAlerts will be of direct use to you.

Accurately Portraying Purpose and Use of Funds

In making a case that a proposed service project, new piece of equipment, or research venture is important, it's sometimes easy to get carried away with our words and exaggerate either the need or our ability to solve the problem. AFT Standard #12 speaks to common ways we can misrepresent aspects of our situation. Because their examples of unethical practice are so succinct and relevant, I quote them here:

1. *Misrepresenting the organization's mission: "The theater's mission is to make the performing arts available to all citizens of the city," when in actuality the price of admission excludes the economically disadvantaged and no free performances or scholarships are offered.*

2. *Misrepresenting facts to justify a case for support: "More than 20 homeless runaways are turned back on the streets every night," when, in fact, those 20 are absorbed by other agencies.*

3. *Misrepresenting the size, breadth and source of support in order to validate cause and case: "The overwhelming majority of neighborhood associations feel this need should be met," when, in fact, presentations at neighborhood association meetings elicited only head nodding from the majority of the audience.*

4. *Misrepresenting anticipated results in order to elicit an emotional response: "Your contribution will save a life" instead of, "You can help save a life."*

5. *Misrepresenting achievements.*

6. *Misrepresenting intent: "If we do not succeed in this campaign effort, we will have to close our doors," when partial success will allow for continuance albeit with reduced staff.*

7. *Misrepresenting philosophy: "We offer service to all needy citizens regardless of race, creed or ethnicity," when, in reality, choices are made along ethnic lines.*

8. *Misrepresenting facts about numbers of clients served, demographics of clients served, activities completed or programs planned.*

9. *Manipulating children, animals, the ill, the elderly, etc.: "The child in this picture was ( ) and has a ninety percent chance of becoming a ( )."*

10. *Creating mailings or other materials that mimic official government mailings or billing notices through deceptive appearance and content of materials. (Code of Ethical Principals and Standards, Association of Fundraising Professions, www.afpnet.org/files/ContentDocuments/CodeOfEthicsLong.pdf)*

Maintaining Confidentiality

Several AFP Standards speak to confidentiality. If you're working in a school, hospital, research lab, or established nonprofit, I'm sure your employee handbook has a lengthy section on the subject. Find that document and reread it. If you're just beginning a new project, consider the information and personal dignity that require respect so you can add appropriate safeguards to your program design. Consider what financial, personnel, and other information you will discover about your agency as you write this grant proposal that warrants confidential treatment.

If you don't have access to a formal confidentiality agreement, download a generic one from the Internet or use these three Standards from AFP as a starting point.

10. *Members shall protect the confidentiality of all privileged information relating to the provider/client relationships.*

17. *Members shall not disclose privileged or confidential information to unauthorized parties.*

19. *Members shall give donors and clients the opportunity to have their names removed from lists that are sold to, rented to, or exchanged with other organizations. (Ibid. AFP Code of Ethical Standards, pages 16, 23, 26)*

All statements say essentially the same thing: Some information is not meant for everyone to know. We're familiar with doctor/patient confidentiality and lawyer/client privileges from watching TV dramas, but once again, we need to consider the specific situations that arise in our particular professions. We need to be aware of laws and regulations governing the use and disclosure of privileged information—and we need to go beyond the letter of the law to ensure the spirit of the law is upheld in the actions we propose.

As a person writing a proposal for a grant, you need to be aware of confidentiality on two levels: program and research issues to include in the proposal, and personal behavior in regard to agency information you have access to. Programmatically, if you are writing a proposal dealing with children, you will surely mention staff training in mandated reporting of suspected child abuse or neglect, locked storage for cumulative records, and conditions under which information can be released to authorities and other programs. In a research grant involving clinical trials, you will include information on how you will ensure informed consent and privacy, as well as confidentiality. Even seemingly traditional ethical protections, however, need to evolve as society changes. In an article in the *British Medical Journal* (www.bmj.com/cgi/content/full/323/7321/1103), Gunther Eysenbach, a senior researcher in the Department of Clinical Social Medicine at the University of Heidelberg, points out that Internet communities such as mailing lists, chat rooms, newsgroups, and discussion boards on web sites are rich sources of qualitative data for health researchers. He points out, however, that most members of these communities do not expect to be research subjects. He reminds researchers to seriously consider whether their research is intrusive and has potential for harm, whether the venue is perceived as "private" or "public" space, how confidentiality can be protected, and whether and how informed consent should be obtained. You need to ask the same questions about your proposed activities.

Turning to personal ethics, if I have the slightest indication that salaries and working conditions are sensitive issues, I suggest someone from the agency I am working for prepare the actual budget while I use only job titles, percentages of time to be spent on the project and job duties for the narrative. On the other hand, I am firm about receiving information regarding financial and programmatic mishaps agencies have experienced in the past 10 years before I accept an assignment. I certainly do not share the information with others, nor do I include it in a proposal, but it's imperative I know everything a potential funder may know (or may have heard on the grapevine). If I know an organization is recovering from a scandal concerning misuse of funds, I need assurance for both myself and potential funders that the situation has been corrected and procedures are in place to prevent any repetition of the actions. I won't mention the scandal in the narrative, but I will add an extra paragraph or two about fiduciary policies, procedures, and safeguards, rather than using my generic phrase about following accepted accounting procedures.

Confidentiality on a personal level also means I need to curb my storytelling around relatives and friends. It may be exciting to receive a sizeable grant from a well-known celebrity, but if he or she requests anonymity, I need to respect that promise. Similarly, when a major corporation decreases the amount of charitable contributions, I can't advise friends to shift their stock portfolios on my assumption that the company is in trouble. Most examples are not that dramatic of course, but you get the idea.

Finally, a seldom remembered, but vital aspect of confidentiality is respecting donor requests.

- Don't keep information about prospective donors and funding sources that they would not be willing to share if asked.
- When a patron asks that a gift be anonymous, respect his or her wishes and don't publish their name in your newsletter or suggest they be the subject of a feature story in the newspaper. Add special safeguards to all records pertaining to anonymous donors so other staff members do not inadvertently make a blunder.
- And as, AFT recognizes, it's vital to give donors and program participants an easy way to delete their names from your mailing lists and other databases when they no longer wish to be involved.

Again, ethical behavior is an extension of good manners where attention to the small details is more important than debating major philosophical issues.

Ensuring Funds Are Used for Designated Purposes

Nothing screams unethical behavior louder than the appearance of misusing donated funds, whether those funds come from the government, foundations, corporations, or individual donors. Notice, I said "appearance." You may not do anything illegal, but if word gets out that a grant to fund a jazz workshop was used to cover the percussion instructor's salary for two months or pay the balance on the grand piano, you're in deep trouble. In addition to humane treatment of clinical subjects and confidentiality, financial issues are the area of greatest ethical concern to most of the public so you must be scrupulous in maintaining transparency in this area.

Because handling money is a heavily regulated process, ethical decisions tend to be more objective and straightforward. Regulations about how to account for and spend money are also more numerous. Basic premises are:

- Documents awarding a grant or specifying donor restrictions are considered legally binding contracts.
- Funds received for a specific purpose must be used for that purpose. If circumstances change, you must negotiate a different allocation of funds *before* you change the budget or spend any additional money.

- Grant funds are restricted funds and must be accounted for separately from other agency grants or operating capital.

- Funds received from grants and contributions are not to unduly benefit any individuals but are to be used for charitable or research purposes.

- Borrowing funds from restricted funds, even temporarily to address cash flow problems, is not acceptable.

- Funders are entitled to regular reports on how grant funds and contributions are used.

In spite of these seemingly obvious statements, regulations change and can be misinterpreted either intentionally or by lack of knowledge. As the person who prepares the grant proposal, you will probably have little influence over how the grant money is eventually managed or mismanaged but you can be cognizant of basic principles and create a realistic program with a feasible budget so that temptations for financial misconduct is minimized.

Avoiding Conflict of Interest

Conflict of interest is closely related to financial issues because people often benefit from inside information or privileged relationships in financial terms. Clearly, hiring your sister's brother-in-law to audit your books without interviewing and considering other applicants is unethical. As Jan Masaoka points out in an article in Blue Avocado (www.blueavocado.org/node/545), the situation is more nuanced than that, especially for nonprofits. There are definite "benefits from interest" when program participants serve on boards of directors, when an expert in a particular field such as disability rights acts as both a board member and a program consultant, or when a staff member's relative owns a building and is willing to provide a reduction in rent. In such circumstances, it makes sense to consider people to have "dual loyalty" rather than "conflict of interest." You can then act appropriately to disclose the situation, ask the person to refrain from voting or otherwise affecting policy or financial decisions in that area, and obtain competitive written bids if major purchases are involved.

If you want to establish or update a conflict of interest policy for your agency, Independent Sector offers an outline of core concepts and discussion points at www.independentsector.org/principle_3_conflicts_of_interest. You can also find a sample in the Blue Avocado article mentioned above.

Protecting Intellectual Property

None of us have purposefully copied someone else's work since we peeked over Mary Kate's shoulder during a math test in third grade. Similarly, none of us would knowingly use the results of another research scientist without attribution or copy another program's proposal verbatim, but ideas and information come from so many sources, we often don't remember if the words and ideas are ours or someone else's. Did the information about childhood obesity come from a conversation with a friend, an article in the newspaper, or something read online? Is it an original source or someone else's interpretation? Admonitions against plagiarism are frequently given, but in this day of ubiquitous information, they are sometimes difficult to follow. Is it important to find the original study, or can you rely on your memory or a scribbled note to include the correct statistics in your need statement? Is citing an author enough, or must you list the journal publication? What's the difference between attribution in a research paper and a grant proposal? What does "based on verified research models" mean when it comes to recognizing intellectual property? There are often no clear-cut lines.

AFP Standard #9 says, *Members shall refrain from knowingly infringing the intellectual property rights of other parties at all times,* so I think it's important to spend time finding original, current sources each time I write a new proposal not only for accuracy and credibility but also for ethical reasons. Someone went to considerable work to gather and analyze data, write a report, or develop a program idea. It is simply good manners to acknowledge their work and to make sure it hasn't been superseded by newer information. AFP also recognizes we don't always know the source of information that seems to be in the public domain by adding a second sentence to the Standard: *Members shall address and rectify any inadvertent infringement that may occur.* Under the pressure of time or in an attempt at summarizing a lengthy or complicated document, it's easy to misinterpret someone's position, credit an earlier researcher, leave a zero out, put the decimal point in the wrong place, or otherwise inadvertently make a mistake. When small errors such as these happen, simply discontinue use of the material, take appropriate steps to apologize, seek permission for continued use, and continue. Since I'm hoping—and assuming—these are the only lapses you will make in protecting the intellectual property of others, here are some strategies to make it easier to avoid those small improprieties.

- **Keep a copy of everything you might possibly use.** Highlight or copy the name and author of the blog, journal, newspaper, or other place you encountered the information. Date it. Add a note regarding its possible relevance or connection to the project. (I know this sounds silly, but you'll wonder why you saved the clipping on community gardens unless you remind yourself it was for the funding source and not the program idea. in a month or two.) In Chapter 14, we'll look at ways of organizing and keeping track of information you may or may not use in various parts of proposals for various funders. Right now, just collect everything that even tangentially relates to program design, community need, research query, funding sources, staff positions, and anything else that catches your eye.

My father reserved the bottom left-hand drawer of his desk for this hodge-podge of preliminary research. When it was difficult to close the drawer, he assigned me to sort it into piles and label file folders to hold them. The system is primitive, but it still works fine for me although I do open a new computer folder for each new project and file gleanings from my web browsing online. When you're ready to create a bibliography, ask for permission to include data, or adapt a successful program to your situation, you'll know whose idea it was. Be sure to date and initial those middle-of-the night ideas you'll have. You've done this before when you've written a major paper or created a to-do list for a holiday party. The only difference is that this collection will probably be more disorganized and have more categories.

- **Read sample proposals early in the process.** Then trust your ability to remember key ideas, format, flow, and other details when it's time to actually write the narrative. As mentioned in the preface, I do not include sample LOIs or proposals in this book because 1) it's too easy and tempting to copy, and 2) each proposal you write must be unique and must sound like you. There is, however, an appropriate time to immerse yourself in sample documents and this is it. Request sample proposals from specific funding sources you have identified or use your favorite search engine to locate samples that match your field of interest. Read them not for content or sections you are tempted to copy, but rather read them to locate resources and to see how other writers deal with difficult topics without overinflating their agency's strengths or weaknesses. How does someone demonstrate their shelter for abused women is worthy of grant funds without putting down similar agencies or stretching their successes rate? Do you include a senior research fellow past his or her prime when you know the main value is name recognition? How do you show community needs without painting a hopeless picture? These are all ethical questions that are addressed indirectly in sample proposals

Don't Chase the Money

Finally, this is more a pet peeve than an ethical issue, but I have serious problems with individuals and agencies who act like chameleons and change their coloration to try to match the latest funding trend. Do you really need the money so badly that you'll stretch your purpose or mission statement out of recognizable shape to obtain it? Don't even be tempted. Not only does it raise ethical questions, but your chances of obtaining such a grant are almost zero. Furthermore, if you do get an award, it will only distract you from the other more important things you are already doing. This sounds fundamental but many individuals and agencies fall into this trap. Yes, you can expand and adapt both the guidelines and your program focus, but don't waste your time or the funder's good graces by applying for something that doesn't fit your core purpose or mission statement. It's just not done in reputable circles.

ACTIVITIES

1. Locate and read a professional code of ethics that applies to your field of work.

2. Identify three areas where the line between ethical and unethical behavior is unclear and develop your own standards for each of them.

3. Find five or more examples of overblown assertions or misrepresentations of facts in unsolicited appeal letters or sample grant proposals and rewrite them to portray a more ethically justifiable position.

4. Identify an area where confidentiality is of prime importance in the implementation of your project, and establish procedures for the use, transfer, and release of privileged information.

5. Learn how restricted funds are managed in your agency or seek guidance in establishing policies and procedures for ethical accounting and reporting practices for new monies.

6. Identify areas where a conflict of interest might arise between a board or a staff member and the proposed project and take appropriate steps to make sure decisions are protected from undue influence.

7. Establish a system for saving and recording information you will use from outside sources.

chapter **7**

Refining Your Program Design

Nobody succeeds beyond his or her wildest expectations unless he or she begins with some wild expectations.

Ralph Charell

The central focus of a proposal for a grant is the program description. It's time, therefore, to refine your program design so you can present a compelling case to partners and funders. You'll continue making decisions about exactly what you want to do and who is going to do it by concentrating on the five sections of the program description in most RFPs and foundation guidelines.

- **Program goals and objectives** transform your purpose into specific, measurable, realistic outcomes.
- **Methods** include program activities, timelines, research protocol, and other implementation steps, including contributions from partners.
- **Staffing** focuses on all full- and part-time program or research staff, administrators, and contracted consultants in both your agency and your partnering organizations.
- **Evaluation** will be structured to measure progress toward and reporting of meeting your objectives.
- **Sustainability** demonstrates the long-term financial continuation of the project.

At the end, we'll consolidate all of this information using the Program Logic Model made popular by Carol Weiss, Joseph Wholey, and others in the 1970s for business applications. Because this is a relatively new model in the nonprofit world and is increasingly required by government agencies and foundations, you may want to read "the end of the book" (or chapter in this case) before you look at the individual steps for getting there.

Defining Goals and Objectives

The goal is the phrase you've been refining since Chapter 2. It's defines the problem you want to solve or actions you want to take in broad, relatively abstract ways that relate to your purpose and vision. A goal for a homeless shelter might be to provide support services and temporary housing for homeless veterans. A goal for a research project might be to understand the genetic basis of graft rejections and differences in transplant outcomes. The music academy might refine the mind map into a goal to remodel the existing facility to offer a wider diversity of programs. The goal of the bark beetle project might be to eradicate the bark beetle from the San Gabriel Mountains. While an agency may have several goals, a grant proposal focuses on one or two.

Objectives, on the other hand, are more specific, tangible things you want to accomplish. They are the stepping stones towards the achievement of your goals so each goal will have several objectives that may focus on either implementation or outcome results. Objectives link the needs you've discovered, the solutions you propose, and the measurement tools you will use in evaluating the success of your efforts so they are the linchpins of your program.

A mnemonic device frequently used in developing objectives is SMART. Although there are variations in the words for each letter (S can stand for specific, simple, significant, or stretching and M can mean measurable, meaningful, or manageable), I prefer Specific, Measurable, Attainable, Relevant, and Time-bound.

- **Specific** means the objective is concrete, detailed, focused, and well-defined. Strong action words, discrete nouns, and qualitative numbers are used. For example, an objective for the music academy's goal to reach new students by expanding the number and variety of program offerings might be: "Ten new six-hour workshops will be offered in ethnic music and ensemble work between September 2011 and June 2012."

- **Measurable** means you are able to gauge the success of your efforts in quantifiable or quantitative terms. The more easily the objective can be measured, the easier making mid-program adjustments, evaluating progress, and reporting to funders and the community will be. "Seventy percent of the students will participate in two or more workshops during the 2011 to 2012 program year."

- **Attainable** also means realistic and feasible because you have or can get the necessary skills and resources to do what you propose in a reasonable amount of time. The percentage in the above example may not be attainable. The music academy might want to change the expectation for currently enrolled students as compared to new students or lower the number to a percent they are sure they can reach. You want to stretch a bit, but you also want to succeed.

- **Relevant** means you listened to your constituents and are providing services or research they consider valuable. If mariachi is more appropriate to the community than polka, be sure to spell this out.

- **Time-bound** means you've set deadlines. While it's tempting to use broad parameters like "program year" or "between September and June" like I did in the examples above, more explicit time constraints are important because they prompt action and create the motivation and sense of urgency that are required to implement a new program. The first objective could be rewritten to read: "Three new workshops or ensembles will be added to the fall schedule beginning in September 2011; four will be added to the winter schedule beginning in January 2012; and three will be added to the spring schedule beginning in April 2012."

When you have the first draft of your SMART objectives written, ask yourself these diagnostic questions:

- Is it clear what will happen and who will be involved?
- How will I know change has occurred?
- Can we do this with the resources we have?
- Will this objective lead to the desired result?
- Do the deadlines fit with other agency commitments?

Don't expect to write SMART objectives in a spare half hour tucked between meetings. They will take time and revision. If you plan to hire outside evaluators, this is a good time to consult with them to make sure you can easily collect appropriate data for them to analyze.

Describing Research and/or Service Methods

Once you know the goals and objectives, your task is to add meat to the bones of your skeleton outline. The RFP and foundation guidelines will contain instructions about the format and content they want in the actual proposal, but the method section is of major importance in research projects because it is where you justify your scientific protocol. You will need to study those instructions carefully and describe your research design in great detail. Because that is not my area of expertise, I suggest everyone begin by following the advice from the tutorial offered by the Foundation Center (http://fundationcenter.org/getstarted/tutorials/shortcourse/methods.html) in which the author recommends answering three basic questions: How, When, and Why.

- **How** are you going to implement your program? For example, how are you going to provide temporary housing and support services to homeless veterans? Where is the housing located? How many people can stay there on a single night? How long can people stay? What kind of support services will you provide? Again, be as detailed and as specific as you can be. Think of all the things that might go wrong—and all the things that will go right—and include them. While this is still your dream project, now is the time to add the hard, cold details of reality. Don't go all over the map, however, but keep your program design tied to the objectives you've just developed.

- **When** will the activities take place? Will you need start-up time to recruit participants, hire staff, or prepare a facility? Is there a sequence to activities? Are events staggered throughout the year? Even if activities are ongoing, you'll need to include evaluation and reporting milestones. Creating a timeline to visually show how program elements are included in the year's flow is a good idea. Even if it's not requested as an attachment to the proposal, it will become a valuable implementation tool to keep you on track once you have the grant money.

- Earlier, I said that I don't believe in questions that begin with the word "why," but this is one place where they are useful. There are many ways to implement a program or research project, and you have made conscious choices about the methods you think will produce the results you want. The funder will want to know your thinking behind those choices, particularly if they are new or unorthodox. You can validate your methods by citing others' research, by using examples of similar approaches that work for other people, by reporting on your successful use of the technique, and even by making the method part of the hypothesis you are testing with the proposed project.

Determining Appropriate Staffing

When you prepared the first draft of the budget in Chapter 3, you listed the number and type of staff you will need to implement your project. In fleshing out the program narrative, let's write a few lines to describe these people in more detail. To start, list the number of staff, whether they will be working full- or part-time, their qualifications and job responsibilities. Include volunteers, as well as paid staff, and don't forget any people you will engage as independent contractors. Also make a note of which people are already on your payroll and which will be hired especially for this project. Each description doesn't need to be extensive. One or two sentences or a table will be enough since you will be asked to include résumés, curriculum vitae, or job descriptions for key positions as part of the appendix, but do spend extra time describing the experience and expertise of the project director if you know who that person will be. A strong project director or principal investigator can help greatly in influencing the decision to fund a project.

Now is also the time to add descriptive words to the project organization chart you created in Chapter 5. You need to describe in some detail several key elements of program administration including:

- Staff supervision and training
- Ongoing program monitoring for quality of service or research and adherence to the proposal objectives
- Shared responsibility and lines of communication among partners
- Financial management
- Evaluation
- Reporting

In many cases, you can condense and edit documents your agency already has. In the case of partnerships or if you are using a fiscal agent, it is extremely important to draft new documents that spell out all parties' roles and responsibilities explicitly. These need to go beyond simple letters of support to become legal, official Memorandums of Understanding (MOU). If money is involved, secure legal advice, but for collaborations of program services, facilities, staff, training, etc., the MOU form shown in this book is sufficient. The following pages show the draft of the master list outlining the types of partners and collaborative contributions they could make to a school readiness program in a Los Angeles County school district. Personal contacts were made with each agency to negotiate the final terms of the MOU. While your list doesn't need to be as long as this one, I firmly believe this application received an extremely high score because of the diversity and depth of the collaborative arrangements.

Agreement #_____

School Readiness Initiative Grants
MEMORANDUM OF UNDERSTANDING

This memorandum of understanding is hereby entered between the two parties indicated below and for the purpose as stated in the scope of work:

SCHOOL READINESS PROGRAM/ CENTER/LEAD AGENCY	COLLABORATION PARTNER/ CONTRACTOR
_____	_____
Contact Person/Title	Contact Person/Title
_____	_____
Address	Address
_____	_____
Telephone _____	Telephone _____
Fax _____	Fax _____
Email _____	Email _____

(Continued)

Scope of Work: Describe in detail the activities or services that the collaborative partner or contractor will provide to the lead agency. Include the rate of pay for the activities/service (a detailed budget is not necessary) that correlates with the amount allocated in the lead agencies budget to the Commission.

_____   _____

Signature   Signature

Lead Agency Representative   Collaborative Partner/
                             Contractor

Date: _____   Date: _____

Memorandums of Understanding (MOUs) are important in specifying the responsibilities for each partner in a collaborate effort so that misunderstandings don't occur if the grant is awarded or denied.

Scope of Works

Sample Scope of Works for Partners
Elementary Schools

- Hold one or more kindergarten open houses for community residents
- Provide training for kindergarten teachers on how to work with children who have and do not have previous group experiences in conjunction with School Readiness Project
- Coordinate family literacy efforts with School Readiness staff
- Provide technical assistance for project-developed readiness materials
- Provide meeting facility for parent and provider meetings and support groups as available
- Select a staff member to serve on the School Readiness Advisory Committee

Secondary High Schools

- Identify pregnant and parenting teens and refer them to School Readiness Project
- Provide CalSAFE facility for extended hours for activities for parents and children to work together on school readiness activities
- Introduce School Readiness staff to community resources used by CalSAFE participants
- Integrate School Readiness case management process with current CalSAFE record keeping
- Provide a member for a Student Study Team for early intervention with at-risk families
- Select a teen to serve on the School Readiness Advisory Committee
- Host voluntary parenting workshops for teens who are not parents but are interested in the subject and/or relatives of parenting teens

Head Start

- Share transition activities, parent involvement strategies, and other current approaches for school readiness currently used with Head Start families as part of orientation for School Readiness Project staff
- Open appropriate Head Start parent workshops to families involved in School Readiness Project
- Provide technical advice for Project-developed readiness materials, book and toy loan purchases, and appropriate community resources
- Select a staff member to serve on the School Readiness Advisory Committee
- Provide meeting facility for parent and provider meetings and support groups as available

Adult School

- Provide parenting, family literacy, child development, and ESL classes for selected groups of participants, i.e., teen parents, grandparents, fathers, guardians, families whose children have special needs, etc., in English and Spanish
- Select a staff member to serve on the School Readiness Advisory Committee

21st-Century Learning Centers

- Identify and refer parents of school-age children who also have children under five to School Readiness Program

- Provide education on benefits of health insurance and enroll families in Healthy Family

- Work with Project staff in training parks and recreation staff in age-appropriate activities for preschool children

- Select a staff member to serve on the School Readiness Advisory Committee

Child-Care Resource and Referral Agency

- Identify licensed child-care centers and family day-care homes in the selected geographic area and refer them to School Readiness Project

- Assist parents with selecting and locating appropriate child care as needed

- Select a staff member to serve on the School Readiness Advisory Committee

- Work with School Reading staff to provide training for providers on school readiness activities, transition between providers and/or kindergarten, nutrition, first aid, child development, and other topics that promote quality out-of-home care

Public Library

- Coordinate current literacy efforts with School Readiness Project

- Publicize School Readiness Project among families with preschool children

- Provide technical assistance for Project-produced school readiness materials

- Provide family tours of library and register Project participants for library cards

- Host joint community information events and/or distribute Project-produced materials

- Select a staff member to serve on the School Readiness Advisory Committee

- Provide meeting space for parent and provider meetings and support groups as available

City Parks and Recreation

- Identify and refer program participants who have preschool children to Project
- Work with Project staff to train recreation staff on age-appropriate activities and strategies for preschool children
- Use of vans and drivers for scheduled family field trips
- Select a staff member to serve on the School Readiness Advisory Committee

All Hospitals

- Provide health education
- Provide physical exams for preschool children in preparation for kindergarten
- Provide immunizations
- Select a staff member to serve on the School Readiness Advisory Committee

For-Profit Clinic

- Work with School Readiness Project on adding locations for mobile clinic to reach greatest number of children from birth to five years in specific neighborhoods
- Provide ongoing medical care for families as appropriate at clinic in Evergreen Park

BCD Hospital

- Provide asthma and respiratory screening, treatment, and education
- Screen family members for chronic illness and refer to appropriate physicians.

KPH Medical Group

- Behavioral pediatrician to screen for attention deficit hyperactive disorder (ADHD) and provide education for parents on disease and its treatment

- Provide wellness education through speaker's bureau
- Provide volunteers through "Hearts at Work" for community project that includes families and focuses on a playground or other project for children under five

Mental Health Clinic

- Provide mental health approach to substance abuse for appropriate parents and/or family members

Asthma/Allergy Breathmobile

- Provide asthma and respiratory screening through mobile unit

Other Potential Collaborators and/or Consultants

- Community college: nutrition education and "Fun, Food and Fitness" program
- WIC: nutrition supplements and education, breast-feeding support
- Stop Gap: teen fathers
- International Center for Transportation: taxi vouchers

Creating Relevant Evaluation

Simply reading the word *evaluation* frightens some people. You may have images of statistics classes with phrases like correlation coefficient and multiple regressions or remember a less-than-flattering performance evaluation on your last job. Whether you call it "assessment," "constructive criticism," or "evaluation," the process always seems to be more painful than you bargained for. I'm not here to change your feelings, but only to offer some tips on how to make the process relevant and useful to your project.

First, don't wait until the end of your project to see what happened. It's important to build evaluation into the ongoing program design so that you can collect and consider information about how well you're meeting your objectives and make modifications in your operations if they are needed. You are probably intending to do this in several areas anyway, so let's look at where ongoing assessment and evaluation already takes place.

- **Financial Accountability:** We talked in the budget section about comparing actual expenditures to the budget, and reporting regularly to the governing board and funders about this area of the operation. Work with an accountant to set up procedures so this happens smoothly and routinely.

- **Program Evaluation:** When you count the number of people who attend a concert, register for swim classes, or accept food from your food bank, you are assessing your program output. When you draw conclusions from that to report in a press release or annual report, you are engaging in a rudimentary form of analysis and evaluation. Program evaluation will play a major role in the evaluation of your project because your SMART objectives will have many measurable dimensions.

- **Participant-related Measures:** In the 1980s, funders started wanting to know that their money was going where it would do the most good. Thus, we started collecting and reporting client data like age, ethnic background, income level, gender, presenting problem, or status prior to service, etc. You'll be asked for this so it's important to collect the information, but its main use is to see if you've missed any obvious groups of potential participants, and/or to tailor programs to meet cultural, economic, social, and other distinguishing characteristics of your clients.

- **Client Satisfaction:** How many surveys have you completed at the end of a seminar that rate the usefulness of the information, speaker's knowledge and presentation style, physical environment, timeliness, etc.? If thoughtfully and carefully constructed, client surveys can be very useful in learning what works and doesn't work at the ground level.

- **Evaluation of Program Outcomes:** This is a new area where we are looking at the difference our projects make. We're not only interested in how many squirming bodies jumped into the swimming pool, we're interested in knowing how many of them actually learned to swim. We want to know if people made and followed a budget after attending a financial literacy workshop. We want to know if there is any difference in the length of time people stay clean and sober if their rehab program was 60 or 90 days.

Yes, funding agencies want to know these things so they can decide where to make their philanthropic investments, but more importantly, this information is vital to your maintaining a quality program that efficiently and effectively does what it says it wants to do. You already have the first draft of your SMART objectives so look at them again to see if they are indeed "measurable"—and change them if they are not. Before you select specific evaluation tools and methods, ask yourself these five questions I've adapted from the *Basic Guide to Program Evaluation* by Carter McNarmara, MBA, PhD, available in the Free Management Library (http://managementhelp.org/evalutn/fnl_eval.htm).

1. What information is needed to make current decisions about a project?
2. Of this information, how much can be collected and analyzed in a low-cost, practical manner?
3. How accurate will the information be?
4. Will the methods get all the needed information?
5. What additional methods should and could be used?
6. Will the information appear credible to the board, funders, and other decision makers?

Choosing Program Evaluation Tools

There are three major types of program evaluation: those that focus on the extent to which programs are meeting predetermined goals or objectives; those that seek to understand the process that makes a program work; and outcomes-based evaluations that ask if you are really doing the right activities to bring about the outcomes needed by the clients. You will probably want to do some of all three.

Goals-based evaluations ask questions like:

- What is the status of the project's progress in meeting its objectives?
- Will the objectives be met according to the timelines we established?
- Does the staff have adequate resources to achieve the goals?
- How can priorities, timelines, and other factors be changed to help us meet our objectives?
- Should any objectives be modified?

Process-based evaluations are useful in portraying how a program truly operates and can include questions like:

- What do employees do to provide services to clients?
- How do clients come into the program, and what is expected of them?
- What is the general process clients go through in the program?
- What does the staff consider to be strengths of the program?

- What do clients consider to be strengths of the program?
- What are typical complaints heard from staff or clients?

Outcomes-based evaluations are increasingly asked for by funders so they should be the main focus of your evaluation efforts. Carter McNarmara, MBA, PhD, has written and spoken extensively in the field of professional and organizational development. In his book *Field Guide to Nonprofit Program Design, Marketing and Evaluation* (Copyright ©2002 Authenticity Consulting, LLC, Minneapolis, Minnesota) he summarizes steps for conducting an outcomes-based evaluation. I have condensed them as a suggested blueprint for you to follow.

1. Identify the major outcomes you want to examine.
2. Pick the top two to four most important ones.
3. For each outcome, specify what observable measures (indicators) will suggest you are achieving that outcome with your clients.
4. Identify what information is needed to show these indicators.
5. Specify a "target" group of clients, i.e., what number or percent of clients will achieve specific outcomes.
6. Decide how to gather the information efficiently and realistically. (Methods can include questionnaires, surveys, checklists, interviews, document review, observation, focus groups, case studies, etc.)
7. Analyze and report the findings.
8. Determine whether the nature of the situation will conform to the methods. (Will clients fill out questionnaires carefully, engage in interviews or focus groups, give permission to examine their files, etc.?)
9. Identify who can administer the method, contract with an outside evaluator, or provide training for someone in-house.
10. Determine how the information can be analyzed.

Books could be written, and have been about evaluation, but I want to close with a look at three more topics before we move on to creating a program logic model.

First, to effectively measure program outcomes as contrasted to program outputs, you will be tapping into four levels of people's behavior. The levels increase in difficulty of measurement but also increase in the specificity of the outcome.

- **Reactions and feelings:** Unfortunately, feelings are often poor indicators of lasting change so you will want to dig deeper than this.
- **Learning:** One of ways to demonstrate that attitudes, perceptions, or knowledge have changed is by comparing these traits at the beginning, at

checkpoints throughout the project, and at the end of an activity or program year. Pre- and post-tests are frequent ways of assessing learning.

- **Changes in skills:** Skills can be anything from learning to do the backstroke to staying within a budget, to handling anger more effectively. Concentrate on the behavioral indicators you want to see and develop ways to measure them.

- **Effectiveness:** Watch for improved performance because of new behaviors learned through the activities.

Next in evaluation issues is the friendly but ongoing debate between folks who swear by qualitative data and those who like to measure things quantitatively. I side with Derek Link, nonprofit consultant and guest writer for the Grant Goddess Blog (http://grantgoddess.blogspot.com), who refers to himself as a hybrid since the data I collect usually falls into both categories. I particularly like his metaphor of viewing results through the data binoculars rather than a data telescope, and I resonate to an example he uses of a child who comes to school on test day.

> The Quant (people who prefer quantitative analysis) will want to examine the child's test score to see whether he has achieved to an expected level, whether he has raised his achievement from previous test administrations, how he compares to his peers, and how his test scores aggregated reflect on the teacher's ability and the school's curriculum and instructional program.

> The Qualits, on the other hand, will want to modify the interpretation of the test score with qualitative information. Perhaps the child arrives hungry because the family was late getting up and she never had breakfast. Perhaps the child is sick or was up all night due to family violence. These qualitative factors impact the ability of the child to score well but are difficult or impossible to quantify.

> In the end, I believe it is a disservice to the process/program/organization to have an imbalanced approach to assessment of results. Start off by asking the right questions. (http://grantgoddess.blogspot.com/2010_02_01_archive.html)

Finally, let me end this section with five pitfalls to avoid from McNamara's book and found in the Free Management Library (http://managementhelp.org/evaluation/fnl_eval.htm)

- Don't balk at evaluation because it seems too "scientific." It's not. Usually the first 20% of effort will generate the first 80% of the plan, and this is far better than nothing.

- There is no "perfect" evaluation plan. It's far more important to do something than to wait until every last detail has been tested.

- Work hard to include some interviews in your methods. Questionnaires don't capture the "story," and the story is usually the most powerful depiction of the benefits of your services.

- Don't interview just the successes. You'll learn a great deal from understanding the mistakes, failures, drop-outs, etc.

- Don't throw away evaluations results once a report has been generated. Like everything else you have collected to this point, they can provide useful information for future projects.

Creating a Program Logic Model

As I mentioned at the beginning of the chapter, condensing all of this information into a format that is comprehensive and easy to access can be accomplished by following the Program Logic Model made popular by Carol Weiss, Joseph Wholey and others in the 1970s. Variations have been developed since then to tailor the language to specific fields, but the basic model is simple, straightforward, and "logical."

INPUTS ➡ ACTIVITIES ➡ OUTPUTS ➡ OUTCOMES

- **Inputs** are the resources we invest in the project, and include staffing, program participants, funding, equipment, and partnerships.

- **Activities** are the processes, tools, events, technology, and actions that make up the program implementation.

- **Outputs** are the products of program activities and are usually measured in terms of the volume of work accomplished, i.e., number of classes taught, participants served, samples studied, pounds of food distributed, or attendance at theatre productions.

- **Outcomes** are specific benefits or changes in participants' behavior, knowledge, skills, status, opinions, etc., as a result of participating in program activities.

- If you want to show long-term change, you can add a fifth step for **Impact** that connects the specific project with the mission of the agency and benefits to the larger community.

In some cases, the lines between categories are blurred but if a logical progression is followed, the result will be comprehensible and useful. For example, the number of patients discharged from a state mental hospital is an *output*, the percentage of those discharged who are capable of living independently is an *outcome*, and the closing of the hospital is an *impact*. Taken all together, they outline your proposed project in a succinct, easily digestible table or diagram.

There are many books and online guides on how to develop and use the tool for your agency that I've included in the Resource section of this book. A working version I've found useful in developing logic models is the one developed by Gary Madden of Inland Empire United Way to implement the 2-1-1 information and referral system in San Bernardino County, California. He has pared the entries to the bare bones in an elegantly simple two-page document so you can not only see the skeleton but can envision the muscles, tendons, and nerves that hold everything together. I've attached it in its entirety with Gary's permission so you can see how much can be communicated with a minimum of words. Of course, something that looks this simple and obvious is very difficult to put together, but this is an excellent model to use as a goal.

PROGRAM LOGIC MODEL

Agency Name: Inland Empire United Way   **Program Name:** 2-1-1 San Bernardino County

Agency Mission: To improve lives by mobilizing the caring power of communities.

Program Goal: The goal of 2-1-1 San Bernardino is to provide timely, effective access to accurate and comprehensive information and referral for the residents of San Bernardino County, and provide coordination support in times of disaster, either natural or deliberate.

Inputs (resources)	Activities	Outputs	Outcomes
Staffing • 2-1-1 Director • 2 Resource Managers • Certified Call Center Specialists *Funding* • United Way • San Bernardino County *Industry-Standard Facility/Equipment* • Call Center • Social services database • Computers • Phone system • Central office switching	Provides information and referral services: • 24 hours per day, 7 days per week • Year-round • Multi-language • Via telephone or Internet • Toll-free • County-wide • Meets industry standards • Connects users who need help *and* those who want to help	• # of calls taken • # of referrals made • # of hits to the online database • # of users connected to a service • # of users receiving needed services	*Participant Outcomes* • Users have increased knowledge of available community resources. • Users are connected with available resources. • Users receive needed services.

(Continued)

PROGRAM LOGIC MODEL (*Cont.*)

Inputs (resources)	Activities	Outputs	Outcomes
Users • Anyone in S.B. County who needs help or wants to help *Partnerships/Collaborations* • Community agencies/organizations • Local disaster/emergency organizations • Other 2-1-1 organizations *Restrictions/Limitations* • Serves San Bernardino County residents only • Must receive official designation from the California Public Utilities Commission (CPUC) • Must work toward Alliance of Information and Referral Services (AIRS) accreditation	• Develops and maintains a comprehensive database of up-to-date social service information. • Develops and maintains a system to track, report, and analyze community needs. • Provides disaster coordination support and responds during times of community crisis.	• # of contacts made with local service providers • # of agencies, programs and services on the database • # of community needs reports produced • # of local crisis/disaster plans prepared • # of local crisis/disaster services and contacts on database • # of partnerships formed with disaster organizations • # of crisis/disasters responded to	*Community Outcomes* • Community agencies are able to provide services more efficiently and effectively.

EVALUATION (MEASUREMENT) PLAN

Agency: Inland Empire United Way   **Program Name:** 2-1-1 San Bernardino County

Outcome	Indicators	Data Source	Data Collection Method	Data Collection Tool	Data Collection Frequency/ Schedule	Sample Size
Users have increased knowledge of available community resources.	• # & % of callers who report they received new resource information from 2-1-1	2-1-1 Callers	Telephone Survey	Webinform database Call Handling	During initial call	All callers
Users are connected with available resources.	• # & % of callers who report they made contact with the service providers referred by 2-1-1 • # & % of callers who report the referral information was correct	2-1-1 Callers	Telephone Survey	Webinform database-Callback Survey	2-10 days after initial call	10% of callers but at least 400 per survey

(Continued)

EVALUATION (MEASUREMENT) PLAN (*Cont.*):

Agency: Inland Empire United Way   **Program Name:** 2-1-1 San Bernardino County

Outcome	Indicators	Data Source	Data Collection Method	Data Collection Tool	Data Collection Frequency/ Schedule	Sample Size
Users receive needed services.	• # & % of callers who report they received assistance from a service provider referred by 2-1-1	2-1-1 Callers	Telephone Survey	Webinform database-Callback Survey	2-10 days after initial call	10% of callers but at least 400 per survey
Community agencies are able to provide services more efficiently and effectively.	• # & % of community agency representatives who report that they use 2-1-1 to refer clients to other needed services • # & % of community agency representatives who report that they save time in referring clients to other services by using 2-1-1 • # & % of community agency representatives who report that their information on the 2-1-1 database is correct • # & % of callers that report that they are receiving accurate referrals from 2-1-1	Community agencies on 2-1-1 database	Telephone Survey	Survey	Annually	Random sample of agencies (10%)

Ensuring Sustainability

Finally, we need to address the matter of how your project will continue after the grant expires. The funders will look at your financial statements to see if you are in a healthy enough position to continue on your own but they will also ask for your specific plans for sustainability. It is not enough to simply say "ongoing expenses will come from the agency's operating budget and individual contributions." You need to be much more specific. Will you designate a percentage of the annual appeal to this project? Can you charge modest fees for the services under the grant and increase them each year thereafter? Will you establish a new special event with the proceeds reserved for activities now supported by the grant? Will you combine this project with other services to form a smaller but more efficient and effective program? Are you cultivating an individual donor who might underwrite the project? Funders do not expect you to have a crystal ball that tells you exactly where new funds are coming from, but they do want to know you have seriously considered the subject.

While sustainability is not listed on most logic model charts, you might add a column on yours to close down this phase of preparing to write a proposal and implement a new project. If worse comes to worse, you have the beginnings of an action plan for alternative funding.

ACTIVITIES

1. Refine two goals for your proposed research or community project.

2. Develop three or four SMART objectives for each goal.

3. Get feedback from someone in your agency or field of study to see if the objectives are specific, measurable, attainable, relevant, and time-bound. Revise them as needed.

4. Create a staffing chart that shows the number of full- and part-time staff, volunteers and independent contractors who will implement the proposed project. Describe their major responsibilities and if they currently are involved with your agency.

5. Write several paragraphs describing how the project with be administered, paying particular attention to ongoing staff and program supervision, financial management, project evaluation, and reporting.

6. Develop a master list of potential partners and what each might contribute to the project.

7. Add a short paragraph to each objective to show how you will evaluate its desired outputs and outcomes.

8. Create a program logic model to outline the inputs (resources), activities, outputs, and outcomes for your project.

9. Sketch two or three ways you plan to sustain the project when the grant expires.

chapter **8**

Focusing on Foundations

Wealth is what you take from the world; worth is what you give back.
Dr. Mark Goulston

Looking for Funds

Now that your dream has a tangible shape, the backing of people who are important to its success, and words to describe its importance, it's time to see where you might get money to make it a reality. Grants are sought for three major reasons: general operations, programs, and capital expenditures.

- **General operating funds** support the daily, ongoing expenses of an organization or individual. These include such items as salaries, materials and supplies, facility rental or upkeep, utilities, transportation, staff training, and marketing. Traditionally, foundations have expected agencies to take care of ongoing activities and structures while they focus on program development and innovative projects. Recently, however, a growing number of foundations have begun offering multiyear **capacity building grants** for strengthening agency infrastructure, a close cousin to operating needs. These include new ventures like creating a paid fund development staff position; expanding a donor base; upgrading computer hardware, software, and online presence; or mounting an outreach campaign.

Occasionally **planning grants** are available to support work on developing a change in direction or the establishment of a major new program emphasis. This type of grant allows you to research community needs, visit programs similar to one you're considering, consult with experts, involve constituents in the program design, and do other planning activities to move a nebulous idea to an organized project ready for implementation.

Usually, operating grants are the most difficult grants to obtain but two changes in recent years are worth noting. In 2004, the board of Independent Sector unanimously endorsed a statement encouraging foundations to pay "the fair proportion of administrative and fundraising costs necessary to manage and sustain whatever is required by the organization to fund that particular project." Within two years, foundation grants for overhead costs grew by 6.7 percent which signals that foundations realize an agency needs to provide electricity, volunteer management, custodial services, and other costs that are usually considered overhead expenses. Second, when the economic downturn occurred in the latter part of the last decade, some foundations changed their priorities to include emergency funds to replace canceled government contracts and/or increased demands for services. Many observers feel these changes will permanently increase funds available for general operating purposes.

• Program funds are defined as "money earmarked for a specific, connected set of activities with a defined beginning and end, explicit objectives and a predetermined cost." This is by far the largest category with research projects, social service programs, cultural events, educational projects, and a host of other activities considered "programs." Research funds may be multiyear grants, but other program monies are usually restricted to a single year. All funds are restricted to the program or project described in the proposal so you can't say you're going to fund wellness activities for seniors and buy new computers for the office. You can, however, include computers for program participants in your application if you define wellness very broadly to include computer literacy as part of reducing isolation for the frail elderly. You can also write a capacity-building request for office computers to streamline accounting and record-keeping activities.

Program grants are sometimes specifically designated as **seed money** to fund the beginning phase of a new program until it is self-supporting and/or can prove its effectiveness. These grants may be for more than one year with decreasing support each year. For example, a grant to establish a spaying program for feral cats may pay for three-quarters of the total expenses the first year, half the second, and one-quarter the third year so the agency has time to develop other funds to sustain the program.

Demonstration grants are another specialty type of program grants. These grants are made to establish an innovative program which, if successful, serves as a model to be duplicated by others. Before applying for a demonstration grant, be sure you have the resources and abilities to evaluate, provide training, and replicate all aspects of the project for an indefinite time. If these elements are in place, when the demonstration project is established, you can apply for **dissemination grants** to publish workbooks, hold workshops, and take other steps to teach others how to copy your program.

- **Capital campaigns** are extensive, multiyear fundraising drives that combine grants with large individual contributions and pledges to finance a major project, such as building a new facility or renovating an old one, establishing an endowment fund or launching a major new program area. You may see these listed colloquially as **bricks and mortar** funds since many involve building buildings. Many foundations make **challenge** or **matching grants** for capital campaigns, whereby they agree to match an amount you raise from other sources. The matching ratio can vary, as can the minimum and maximum amounts.

Matching funds are not restricted to capital campaigns, however. Most government grants require a percentage of the project be raised from nongovernmental sources, and both operating and program grants usually fund only a portion of the total amount needed for the project. We'll explore various ways to raise these funds in Chapter 10.

Finding Funding Sources

Grant makers come in as many varieties as the type of requests they fund. Fortunately, the methods of finding funding sources and the process of requesting funds are surprisingly similar whether you are applying to a foundation, corporation, or government funder. The process is also the same regardless of the amount of funds you are requesting. You may be looking for a small grant ($500 to $10,000) to start a project, provide supplies for a single classroom or program focus, or fill a gap in a continuum of services. Maybe you are more interested in larger grants to fund a major research project, duplicate a program in several locations, or build a new facility. Generally, smaller grants will be made by foundations and corporations while larger grants come from national foundations and the government, but this is not always the case so you'll want to look at a wide array of funding options.

Foundation Funding

The word *foundation* has no legal meaning in and of itself. In common usage, however, we use it to mean *a nongovernmental, nonprofit organization that serves the public good primarily through the making of grants to other nonprofit organizations.* Foundations are also distinguished by having a principal fund managed by its own trustees or directors. Differences between public and private foundations can be found in their mission, IRS designation, source of funds, and reporting requirements. The most important distinction between private and public foundations is that all private foundations must make charitable expenditures of approximately 5 percent of the market value of their assets every year. This requirement guarantees there will be an ongoing funding stream from a private foundation even though the amount available for distribution may vary from year to year.

Regardless of public or private designation, there are more than enough foundations with sizeable assets to fund your project. The National Center for Charitable Statistics reports there are 88,879 private foundations with over $566 trillion dollars in total assets who registered with the IRS in 2009 and 2010. The Foundation Center lists over 98,000 U.S. foundations and corporate donors and over 1.7 million grant opportunities. Your task is to find which ones give grants to your geographic area and match your field of interest.

Foundations can be separated into five categories with each having a slightly different focus. Knowing the distinctions will help you narrow the field and will influence the approach you will take in writing your proposal.

- **Community foundations** are public foundations that combine and manage funds from many different donors to make grants in a specific geographic region. Usually the donors' funds remain intact and grants are made from the interest on investments. Community foundations hold many designated funds and focus on local issues, so it's particularly important to follow their work in your community and become acquainted with their staff. You can find the community foundations in your area by entering your zip code in the "Community Foundation

Locator" maintained by the Council of Foundations at www.cof.org. Go to "those we serve" on the tool bar at the top, then find "community foundations" from the pop-up menu and scroll to the bottom of the page to find the locator map. There are approximately 650 community foundations in the United States.

- **Corporate foundations** are private foundations that derive their grant-making funds primarily from the contributions of a profit-making business. The mission of the foundation and the goals of the corporation are usually complementary, but the organizations remain legally separate. The Foundation Center reports corporate grant-making foundations have roughly doubled since 1990 with 2,600 foundations distributing $4.4 billion in 2007. To maintain the integrity of your research and be true to your mission statement, you will want to make sure your goals match the corporate goals.

- **Family foundations** are independent private foundations whose funds come from members of a single family. Family members often serve as officers and play a major role in grant-making decisions that are frequently very personal. Some have grown very large like the Ford Foundation, but most are considerably smaller and make smaller, more local grants. Because they are sometimes less sophisticated than other foundations and not as visible, locating them can be a challenge. However, once a personal relationship is formed, family foundations sometimes "adopt" local groups for multiyear funding.

- **Limited-purpose foundations** restrict their giving to one or very few fields of interest such as higher education, health, or a specific religious cause. Often specific colleges, universities, hospitals, or research centers are named in the guidelines and proposals from other grant seekers are not accepted. If you are seeking a scholarship or fellowship, these are often rich sources of funding. Consult professional journals and ask principal investigators at your local college or university for help in finding appropriate limited-purpose foundations in your field of study.

- **Operating foundations** are private foundations that use the bulk of their income to run charitable programs of their own. They make few, if any, grants to outside groups. For example, the Doris Duke Foundation for Islamic Art (DDFIA) is an operating foundation funded by the larger Doris Duke Foundation to promote the study and understanding of Islamic arts and cultures. DDFIA's primary focus is operating Shangri La,

Doris Duke's home in Honolulu that today houses her collection of Islamic art. DDFIA also awards some grants to groups in the New York area through the Building Bridges Program that seeks to improve understanding between the United States and Muslim societies through the arts, media, and cross-cultural education and exchanges.

Finding Foundation Funding

Like so many other aspects of our personal and professional lives, grant seeking moved online during the first decade of the 21st century. All major foundations and many, many smaller ones post guidelines and accept applications online. Many also list current and past grant recipients so you can get a sharper picture of what they do and do not fund. If you already have ideas about a foundation that funds programs like the ones you are proposing, go directly to their web site. If, on the other hand, you are starting from scratch or want a larger list, keep reading.

As a personal research project, I asked random people attending a nonprofit grant seeking seminar where they looked for grant sources. The two most frequent suggestions were the Foundation Center and Google. As mentioned earlier, the Foundation Center lists over 98,000 U.S. foundations and corporate donors and over 1.7 million grant opportunities.

The effectiveness of a Google search depends, of course, on your choice of key words. A search for "California Foundations" produced 53,900,000 options and no real information about what they funded. When I entered "art education grants in Oregon," however, the list contained only 262,000 options and the first page had six entries that merited investigation including the Oregon Education Association, and the Oregon Arts Commission. Searching for "foundations that fund diabetes research" shortened the list still further (120,000), and produced ten relevant options on the first page. While you may have thought of the Juvenile Diabetes Research Foundation and the American Diabetes Association on your own, were you aware the Iacocca Family Foundation and the Kauffman Foundation invest substantially in diabetes research?

Traditionally, grant seekers first consult the Foundation Center (http://foundationcenter.org), which is actually a very good beginning since it's the hub of information about large and small, public and private, community and celebrity foundations, as well as every other topic that relates to foundations that you can imagine. If you're connected to a university, hospital, or research center, ask about access to their subscription service since it's pricey for an individual. When you have a clear focus of the foundations you want to research, you can subscribe for a single month and access all the information on the site. If you're just starting out, there are several ways to take advantage of their free and relatively inexpensive resources.

- Use the variety of free search tools, tutorials, downloadable reports, and other information on their web site. I suggest you browse the "get started" section, try a few search words and generally get acquainted with the site on a day when you have some time. It's not difficult to navigate but there is so much information at a national and broad policy-making level that it's easy to become overwhelmed. For a useful list of nonprofit resources including links to other funding search engines, check out http://foundationcenter.org/gainknowledge/nonprofitlinks/fund.html.

- If you know the name of the foundation, you can find contact information and IRS 990-PF forms at http://lnp.fdncenter.org/finder.html. The IRS forms provide basic data on income, assets, number of grants made, and sometimes a list of grant recipients for each fiscal year. To get the more detailed information you'll need before you write a proposal, you'll need access to information reserved for subscribers or go directly to the foundation's web site, but we'll cover that later.

- Visit one of the foundation's five regional library/learning centers (New York City; Washington, DC; Atlanta; Cleveland; and San Francisco) or connect with one of the 425 cooperating collections that offer free access to all their information resources and educational programs. Their on-site and online librarians are very knowledgeable and most helpful.

- Subscribe to two of their free newsletters. *RFP Bulletin* lists both foundation and government requests for proposals arranged by fields of interest with the posting and deadline dates, a synopsis of the grant focus, and a link to the funding agency for complete information. A random RFP Bulletin listed grants under aging (1), arts and culture (5), athletics and sports (1), children and youth (1), health (2), international affairs (1), medical research (2), and science and technology (1). *PND Connections* provides background information about the field of philanthropy in general by printing excerpts from news articles, interviews with funders, and program models.

Beyond the Obvious

Return as often as you like to these two reliable sources for locating foundations and other funding opportunities, but also look in other directions. With technological tools so readily available, other foundation search engines and foundation funding alerts have appeared that cater to geographic areas or niche grant seekers. Some sites are designed for a specific audience, whereas some are very general. They are all configured differently and tend to be relatively informal, so you'll need to sample several to discover which work best for you. Since many offer free newsletters simply by registering, you can keep abreast of appropriate funding opportunities in your specific area of interest without wading through pages of irrelevant postings. Here are a few not listed by the Foundation Center that I've found helpful.

- **Regional and state directories** may take a little detective work to locate because they are published in a variety of formats by a variety of people. In some states, they are produced by regional associations of grant makers (RAGs); in others, the attorney general's office produces them, and in many states, they are created by small publishing houses or commercial fundraising firms. Some include profiles of corporate giving and/or church-sponsored, government, and collaborative funding. Some simply provide minimal contact information, whereas the better directories add application procedures, eligibility restrictions, funding cycles, annual report summaries, etc. You can find a directory of RAGs at www.givingforum.org.

- *Duke University funding opportunities* (http://researchfunding.duke.edu) provides an extensive database that focuses on science and academia. You can check out weekly postings of open funding opportunities by discipline and deadline and then click on individual postings for a synopsis, eligibility details, award amounts, and announcement links. An advanced search function links you to Grants.gov for federal grants, as well as databases maintained by COS (Community of Science), IRIS (Illinois Research Information Services), and FDO (Foundation Directory Online).

- **Grants Net Express** offered by *Science* magazine of the American Association for the Advancement of Science is geared to scientists-in-training in biomedical research and science education. You need to register but it's free at http://grantsnet.org.

- **Grant Gopher** (www.grantgopher.com/) caters to the nonprofit world with a free weekly emailed bulletin that includes some information on available grants A full year's membership is $50, which entitles you to post independent requests for funds and technical assistance as well as receive more detailed grant information.

- **Discount School Supply** (www.discountschoolsupply.com) seems an unusual place to look for money, but they have an excellent free database of funding resources for all kinds of educational purposes and organizations including preschool, public, private, and faith-based elementary and secondary school and after-school programs. Because it's primarily a school supply catalog, you need to click on "resources" and scroll down to My School Grant^{SM}.

- **Open Directory** (www.dmoz.org) is a giant collection of miscellaneous information but if you type "funding for _____" in the search box at the top, you can discover unusual funding sources for categories like gay and lesbian services (www.lgbtfunders.org), film-making (www.cinereach .org), and youth sports (www.la84foundation.org) that are often difficult to find elsewhere.

Serendipity

Another valuable way of finding funding sources is to follow the paths you discover in professional journals or when you're browsing online. While it's not the most efficient method of finding funding sources, it's amazingly effective. When you are mindlessly following a personal interest, you're apt to find at least a few like-minded souls who are willing to fund your project. That's how I discovered the **Great Lakes Directory** (www.greatlakesdirectory.org) filled with foundations that fund environmental causes in the Midwest and C. Hope Clark's **Funds for Writers** (www.fundsforwriters.com) that includes fellowship and grant opportunities with contests, freelance jobs, and good advice for those of us who write. Following one of Hope's postings I discovered **Mira's List** (http://misraslist.blogspot.com) that specifically "provides information on upcoming grants, fellowships and residencies for artists, writers, composers, and media artists." If you gain nothing else, you'll discover a new twist for your project to set it above the usual proposals and thereby increase your chances for being awarded a grant.

Finding Family Foundations

Unfortunately there is no central directory or easy way to find family foundations. They are often small, local, and just below the radar. Some have pooled their resources into regional community foundations and can be accessed by reading that group's annual report and talking with their program staff. It's perfectly acceptable protocol to phone a community foundation and say, "I'm looking for funds to expand the number of books and videos for our research library for child-care providers. Does the Northside Community Foundation manage funds that might be appropriate or do you know of family foundations in our area who might be interested in such a project?"

Trust officers in banks, estate attorneys, and other financial planners often know of family foundations. While they are bound by client confidentiality, if you have developed a relationship with someone in that profession, they are often willing to mention your cause to their clients. It doesn't happen often, but what a thrill it is when someone on the phone says, "My name is Yolanda Jackson and I'm the administrator of the Jackson Family Foundation. I understand from my attorney that you are searching for funds to provide services for homeless teens. Our foundation supports the Elm Street Shelter, and I would be interested in learning more about your programs. Are you available tomorrow afternoon at 2:30?" You never know when or if this will ever happen to you, but it is one of the benefits of being known in the community and meeting a broad range of people in different professions. You can start the process by asking to speak to the trust officer the next time you go to your bank or by looking for a financial planner at the next Chamber of Commerce meeting. I think you'll be pleasantly surprised by their approachability and their interest.

The final and easiest way to find a family foundation is by carefully reading the local newspaper and the programs you receive at concerts, plays, and other community events. Sometimes family foundations will be acknowledged as a major donor, sometimes they are hiding in the smaller print, and sometimes they will be featured in a congratulatory advertisement. Although I'm jumping ahead in my story, let me point out that reading the newspaper and other groups' programs is also the best way of locating individual donors. After a month or two, you'll start recognizing names because generous people give to more than one cause. Don't—and let me repeat that in capital letters—DON'T—call or phone them and ask for money. You have lots of research and cultivation to do, but the first step is identifying the possibilities. Your task at this point is to start an alphabetical file of "Potential Local Funders" and add to it as frequently as you can. Who knows when you'll discover a fabulous resource in your own backyard?

ACTIVITIES

1. Sketch three ideas for grants you would like: one for capacity building, one for planning, and one (or more) for program development.

2. Find a community foundation that serves your geographic area and discover at least two ways they can be a resource for you.

3. Enter your specific field of interest in your favorite search engine and locate six or more potential foundations.

4. Become familiar with the Foundation Center web site and find three or more useful and relevant resources.

5. Find and register for at least one specialized service that provides grant alerts.

6. Follow a web browsing trail until it leads to a potential project idea or funding source.

chapter **9**

Demystifying Government Funding

Any "premature impact of an aircraft with terrain" is a "crash."
Federal Aviation Administration

Yes, the government speaks and writes a language that sometimes puzzles, amuses, and amazes those of us who live outside the Beltway. Their often tortuous and convoluted language also makes deciphering federal and state requests for proposals a challenge. Still, this is where major money for research, education, and health and social services resides so we need to become comfortable with the system and learn the lingo.

When someone talks about receiving funds from the government, they usually mean federal grants because that's where the big dollars are and that's where most government money originates. Unfortunately, federal funds are highly competitive, carefully scrutinized, and burdened with regulations and paperwork. If you're just beginning to do independent research or are seeking funds for a small agency that has been in existence for only a few years, it's smarter to start with more local entities. We'll look at how to access larger federal and state funds later in the chapter, but first, let's begin at home.

There are two primary avenues to explore in the town or city where you live: a direct grant under the Community Block Development Grant (CBDG) program and a partnership with a city department or the local school district.

- **Community Block Development Grants** have been around since the 1974 Housing and Community Development Act was passed to strengthen the vitality of urban communities. Most of the money goes for housing rehabilitation, and infrastructure projects like street repairs, and sewer and water lines but as much as 15 pecent can be used for public service programs. Projects must meet an urgent need, benefit low- and moderate-income families and eliminate slums and blight. Each community defines these criteria separately, and many of the definitions are very broad. Typical programs that are funded include senior nutrition, adult literacy, homeless services, sexual assault and domestic violence programs, after-school activities, and the renovation of community centers. Because the money is granted locally, the process tends to be rather informal. Of course, it's influenced by local politics, but if you are visible in the community and maintain a strong networking effort, you can have a direct effect on the decision makers. Typically grant applications are accepted in the fall, awards are made in the spring, and funds are released July 1st. Check with your city's planning department for specific information.

- **Partnerships with city departments and the local school district** are also viable means of funding programs. Youth and senior activities sponsored by colleges, museums, religious organizations, and nonprofit agencies in conjunction with the police, fire, and park and recreation departments, library, and all levels of public and private schools are common. So are "one-stop shops" for the homeless that bring together physical and mental health providers, housing and food services, and social work research. Consider eco-scapes that combine neighborhood organizations with city services, volunteer opportunities, and maybe the animal shelter's dog park. You'll need to be persistent and creative, but the possibilities are endless.

Another source of cash grants are **regional groups like water, transportation, and economic development agencies**, especially for rural areas. Again, the funds are relatively small, but the competition is less intense and the application procedure is simpler than going for county, state, or federal funds. Water and power bureaus can fund everything from community education projects and wildlife inventories to engineering models and demonstration gardens. Fourteen teachers in Southern California who explored this option received $500 grants for water-related classroom activities from a consortium of 12 local water agencies that also sponsors an annual high school video contest and conducts teacher workshops. In another example, a community center providing job retraining for unemployed workers secured a multiyear Homeland Security grant administered by a local transportation board to screen and train long-distance truck drivers in transporting hazardous waste materials. Finally, take a page from artists and scientists who find project collaborators and research subjects in penal institutions to explore research, therapeutic, life skills, and fine arts projects within the prison system.

Don't forget to investigate departments within your **county government's structure.** While some may not be as generous as the San Bernardino County (California) Grants Office, where I live, they all have access to resources they may be willing to share. With the support of members on the Board of Supervisors, the San Bernardino Grants Office conducts yearly mini-conferences on funding for nonprofits and small business firms, offers technical advice, and provides frequent updates of geographically appropriate grant funding opportunities to nonprofit agencies through a contract with **GOStream™**. Many of their resources, such as sample proposals and grant writing hints, are available to everyone at www.sbcounty.gov/grantsoffice.

A few states offer similar services. For example, the Maryland Governor's Grants Office (www.grants.maryland.gov) is recognized as a "best practice" by the National Governors Association for going beyond its original mission of increasing funding to the state and reducing audit findings. Their range of activities now includes better state grant opportunities, linking foundations to nonprofits, and grants management training that is easily accessible.

Finally, an important resource for individual artists is the Arts Council in each state. There are different names—Artist Trust in Washington, Massachusetts Cultural Council, Tennessee Arts Commission, etc.—but all are listed at www.nasaa-arts.org. The **California Arts Council** (www.cac.ca.gov/enews.index/php) publishes a regular newsletter that announces their own grants and programs but also provides summaries of other grant opportunities in the arts and culture arena. Register with the Council in your state to learn about and support the arts even if you never use one of the funding postings.

Time to Access County, State, and Federal Funds

If you are seeking funds for direct service in areas like counseling, substance abuse treatment, and child care or research in any specialized scientific field, you will want to eventually secure larger, ongoing grants from federal, state, and county sources. The vast majority of these grants originate in Washington, DC, before they are passed down to states, which further divide them into county grants. For this reason, the application and funding process for all three levels tends to follow federal procedures, regulations, budget hearings, and timelines. Of course, state and county procedures, regulations, budget hearings, and timelines are added to the mix, so you'll want to take advantage of any training (often called bidders conferences) the state or county offers.

All government grants are awarded in two categories: "formula" grants and "project" grants. (Yes, there are also designated grants and contracts known informally as "pork barrel" and "earmarks," but they are outside the realm of this book because you need to be a large organization and/or have considerable political influence to obtain them.)

- **Formula grants** are based on a set amount for each participant and are paid after services have been provided. If you follow educational funding, you know local schools pay very close attention to attendance. This is because their funding is based on average daily attendance (ADA). The same principle, with varying mathematical formulas, applies to prisons, mental health services, and medical reimbursements. While most formula grants are restricted to other government agencies, some like substance abuse prevention and treatment, counseling services, and child care are available for community organizations.

  Formula grants present several fiscal challenges. Because you are reimbursed for services already provided, you need to have substantial cash reserves to fund operating expenses for at least three months. Second, if you plan your budget on a certain level of enrollment, you must maintain that enrollment at all times to receive your budgeted allocation. If someone drops out or is terminated, you will not receive funds for that "slot" until a replacement has been found. Finally, formula funds are carefully audited, and you may be required to return money received for billings judged to be in error.

  Having said this, formula grants are the lifeblood for Head Start, state preschools, recovery programs, food pantries, domestic violence and sexual assault programs, homeless shelters, and other social service providers because once an initial contract is obtained, ongoing funds are relatively secure. Many formula grants are funded on a three- to five-year cycle with yearly updates. Though agencies do lose county, state, and federal contracts because of budget cuts or program mismanagement, warning signals are usually evident well in advance, which allows you to search for alternative funds.

- **Project grants** fund specific research and service programs the current administration and legislative branches of the government can agree should be implemented. Requests for Proposals (RFPs) and detailed guidelines are published and applications are accepted, reviewed, and ranked by panels. Grants are awarded on your proposal's ranked score and the total amount of funds available. These are highly competitive grants because you are competing against all of the other research projects or social service agencies in your field in your county, state, or the nation.

Accessing Federal Grants Through www.Grants.gov

The key to all national grants is www.Grants.gov because it's the portal to all discretionary federal funds offered by the 26 federal grant-making agencies. While you may gather information from other sites and even submit your application to a specific department, www.Grants.gov is where you will go as your first and last stop.

The site looks remarkably easy to navigate and has instructions and options at every step of the way, but you can easily get lost. Grab a pen and some paper to record sites you want to remember, and follow me on a brief, unofficial tour.

- For a quick search of what grants are currently available, click *New Opportunities This Week* at the bottom of the page. There may be half a dozen or more than a hundred RFPs (Requests for Proposals) listed, depending on the time of year. Because the federal fiscal year runs from October 1 to September 30, most applications are due in May and June so RFPs are posted in April and May. Yes, that's a tight timeline, but that is one of the challenges of securing a federal grant.

- If you find an entry that looks feasible, copy both the title and the funding number (Migratory Bird Project Support: Monitoring, Assessment, Conservation: FWSR2-MBP-LEAD-FY2010). We'll come back to them later.

- First we're going to search a bit further. Go back to the www.Grants.gov home page and click *Grant Search* under *For Applicants* in the *Quick Links* box on the right. Notice you have four choices: Basic, Category, Agency, or Advanced Search.

- Choose *Basic* and enter a word that broadly describes what you're interested in researching like "botany" or "autism" or "asthma." You'll be presented with a chart that has a wide range of funding opportunities arranged in no apparent order. Some are clearly earmarked (Herpetological Study at NAS Fallon, NV); some have dates that have long passed (05/08/2009: Addressing Asthma from a Public Health Perspective); and some are due next week. Browsing a bit, however, gives you a sense of the kind of projects that receive funds and the wide variety of sources within the federal government. If you sort by *Close Date*, you can get a head start on what's in the pipeline that might be relevant. If you find something that looks interesting, jot down the title and funding number.

- If you haven't found anything that interests you yet, *Browse by Category* next. Where do you suppose we can find information about our botany/autism/asthma interests? Agriculture? Education? Health? Try one and see what you find. When I looked under "Health," I found 1,126 options in the same jumbled chart format. Sort by date to see if you can find a grant title and funding number to explore. Clearly this is not an efficient way of finding a funding source, but again, it demonstrates the variety of projects and sources of funds.

- There's one more place I want to take you before we use our magic funding number. The *Advanced Search* option is a horse of a different color from most advanced search engines. With some trial and error, I discovered the best results by entering: "Keyword," "Open Opportunities," "Nonprofit with a 501(c)(3)," "All Funding Activity Categories," "All Agencies," and "Grant." Doing this, I discovered one title for asthma, four for autism, and none for botany. The results were the same when I chose "Public/Private Institutions of Higher Learning" as the eligibility requirements. On a lark, I entered "obesity" as the key word and discovered 31 options with deadlines between June 22, 2010, and March 1, 2012. Yes, the federal government follows trends in funding cycles.

Now let's take the funding number you've found and see where it leads us. Find your way back to the *Grants Search* page and type the funding number into the appropriate box. Voilà! You'll find a synopsis of the funding opportunity. Read it carefully to see if it is still of interest and if you qualify. The migratory bird grant I mentioned earlier said:

THIS IS A NOTICE OF INTENT TO AWARD TO A SINGLE SOURCE; THERE IS NO "FULL ANNOUNCEMENT" ASSOCIATED WITH THIS NOTICE. This Notice is NOT a request for competitive proposals. In accordance with Department of the Interior guidance (505 DM 2.14) the U.S. Fish and Wildlife Service (Service) intends to make a single-source award of $30,000.00 to Stephen F. Austin State University under a modification to an existing cooperative agreement between the recipient and the Service.

In other words, this path came to a screeching halt for me—and yes, this happens frequently because once you do get funding, it's relatively easy to continue the "cooperative agreement." If your result stated that a full announcement was available, bookmark the site because we'll demystify a federal funding announcement in Chapter 11. If you need to look further to find an appropriate grant, check the new opportunities section every few days until you find an announcement of interest that has an open competitive process.

Federal Agencies That Award Grants

Before we completely leave Grants.gov, let's explore those 26 agencies that provide funds to community agencies and research institutions. All of the agencies can be reached from Grants.gov or you can access them individually at the web site following each agency. I suggest you explore a few that are unfamiliar to you because there are some surprising funding sources where you least expect them.

Support for research and development at colleges and universities is concentrated in six agencies that accounted for 95 percent of the total federal research and development funds in 1999, so let's look at those first.

- **National Institutes of Health (www.nih.gov):** Although officially the NIH lies within the Department of Health and Human Services (HHS), it provides over $8 billion in grants each year on its own. Almost 90 percent of the funded projects are in the life sciences, with microbiology and medical sciences receiving the most funds. Psychology, physical sciences, and social sciences share the remaining 10 percent. The NIH uses three major funding instruments (grants, contracts, and cooperative agreements) and four different funding avenues (investigator-initiated research, program announcements [PA], Requests for Applications [RA] and Requests for Proposals [RFP]) so this is not the place for beginners. While much of the material in this book will still be applicable, if this is your first experience with the NIH, find an experienced research colleague as a principal investigator posthaste. This is not something you want to do alone.

- **National Science Foundation (www.nsf.gov):** In second place is the NSF, which annually funds approximately 20 percent ($2 billion) of basic, federally supported college and university research. Its funding is evenly distributed between physical sciences and engineering, with smaller amounts going to environmental sciences, life sciences, computer sciences, and an even smaller percentage going to social and behavioral sciences. An acronym to look for is **STEM**—shorthand for Science, Technology, Engineering, and Math. It's widely used by the NSF and the Department of Education (ED).

- **Department of Defense (www.defense.gov):** While the DOD primarily funds military operations and research devoted to the development, testing, and evaluations of weapons systems, there is still plenty of money available for academic research in engineering, computer, physical, life, and environmental sciences. The DOD recently instituted a New Idea Portal where anyone can request funding for an idea on the selected topic and receive a response within 30 days.

- **National Aeronautics and Space Administration (www.nasa.gov):** Under the Obama administration, NASA is taking a new shape, but graduate fellowships and research opportunities in astronomy, atmospheric sciences, aerospace engineering. and life sciences are still available.

- **Department of Energy (www.energy.gov):** With energy efficiency a buzzword as I write, the DOE has several research initiatives available in fossil, nuclear, wind, and other forms of energy as well as in basic science, advanced computing, biological and environmental research, fusion, high energy and nuclear physics, materials, and medical fields.

- **Department of Agriculture (www.USDA.gov):** Research projects in all phases of plant and animal science, home economics, and food security are supported by competitive grants. In addition, funds are available for rural and community development. Here's where funds for food banks, school meal programs, and nutrition education often originate.

- **Department of Health and Human Services (www.hhs.gov):** HHS is a major granting agency for nonprofits of all kinds because it distributes funds through 11 operating divisions, in addition to the National Institutes of Health (NIH). These include the Administration for Children and Families (ACF), Substance Abuse and Mental Health Services Administration (SAMHSA) and the Administration on Aging (AoA). This is where most people in social sciences will find grants, but do browse some of the other sites because there are always surprises that may open up a new line of research, fund a collaborative partner, or suggest a program variation.

- **Departments of Education (www.ed.gov):** Most ED funds go for Pell grants and local education agencies (LEAs), but it's a good site for exploring potential collaboratons for research and demonstration projects in education, psychology, nutrition, autism, and other special learning needs as well as for after-school programs incorporating art, film writing, music, etc., co-sponsored by nonprofit organizations.

- **Department of the Interior (www.doi.gov):** In addition to managing the National Park Service and several regulatory agencies, DOI oversees the Bureau of Indian Affairs, Bureau of Land Management, Bureau of Reclamation, the U.S. Fish and Wildlife Service, and the U.S. Geological Survey which all have grants programs.

- **Department of Justice (www.justice.gov):** Funds are available for research and community programs in juvenile justice and delinquency prevention, as well as for programs that support survivors of domestic violence, sexual assault, dating violence, and stalking.

- **Department of Labor (www.dol.gov):** Although the name of the program seems to change with every administration, there always seems to be money available to train and retrain youth and adults in multiple categories.

- **Department of Housing and Urban Development (www.hud.gov):** HUD is known for public housing and FHA financing but also includes the Center for Faith-Based and Neighborhood Partnerships and Fair Housing/ Equal Opportunity activities.

- **Environmental Protection Agency (www.epa.gov):** If you're looking for a fellowship or research grant in a field related to environmental science or technology or want to help reduce pollution locally, an EPA grant might fit.

- **Institute of Museum and Library Services (www.imls.gov):** This agency wins my votes for the most user-friendly site for grant seekers created by a federal agency. The Institute's primary function is to serve the nation's 122,000 libraries and 17,500 museums, and it does that by making funding opportunities easy to access, easy to understand, and easy to apply for.

Even if you are not directly involved in a library or museum, visit this web site to explore community engagement, informal learning, and partnership opportunities.

- **National Endowment for the Humanities (www.neh.gov):** This independent grant-making agency of the federal government supports research, education, preservation, and public programs in the humanities.

- **National Endowment for the Arts (www.nea.gov):** The NEA is the largest national source of funds for the arts and offers fellowships in certain forms of literature, jazz, heritage, and opera as well as many programs for non-profit agencies.

Other federal agencies on the list that provide funds for very specialized purposes include:

- **U.S. Agency for International Development (www.usaid.gov):** The USAID helps fund global humanitarian projects with several grant programs for small nonprofits.

- **Corporation for National and Community Service (www.nationalservice .gov):** The CNCS oversees VISTA, Senior Corps, AmeriCorps Learn, Serve America, and similar community service programs (but not the Peace Corps, which is under the Office of Inspector General or OIG).

- **Department of Commerce (www.commerce.gov):** Home site for the U.S. Census Bureau and the National Oceanic and Atmospheric Administration (NOAA).

- **Department of Homeland Security (www.dhs.gov):** DHS and the Federal Emergency Management Agency (FEMA) are almost synonymous these days because of their well-publicized programs like disaster preparedness and emergency response, but there are also opportunities for collaboration with community education, training, and systems improvement projects.

- **Department of State (www.state.gov):** This department handles foreign affairs. Like USAID, the State Department has several grant programs specifically for small nonprofits.

- **Department of Transportation (www.dot.gov):** Many agencies twist letters to create pronounceable acronyms for their funding programs, but DOT wins my votes for their stimulus recovery programs: TIGER (Transportation Investment Generating Economic Recovery). Unfortunately, you have to be a state or regional transportation to qualify for this and most other grants from this department.

- **Department of the Treasury (www.ustreas.gov):** The Treasury bureaus collect, regulate, and monitor money rather than give it away, but this is where you receive your 501(c)(3) tax exemption letter so it's worth a brief visit.

- **Department of Veterans Affairs (www.va.gov):** Funds support medical, employment, housing, and other benefits to military veterans and the organizations that provide them.

- **National Archives and Records Administration (www.archives.gov):** The National Archives are the place to search for "pork barrel" and other quietly granted funds if you're so inclined.

Funding for For-Profit Businesses

Finally, let me say a few words about the **Small Business Administration (SBA)** because it's also a government agency that distributes funds, and those funds cause a lot of confusion. The federal government does *not* give grants to businesses, but it does guarantee business *loans,* and this is where they originate. The following chart adapted from one developed by Deborah Kluge (www .proposalwriter.com) shows the type of loans and who is eligible for them.

Loan Type	Description	Eligibility
7(a) Small Business Loan	Most basic and most frequently used loan—designed to assist for-profit businesses who are not able to get funding from other sources—interest rates vary on loans up to $2 million maximum loan with 25 years term for real estate and 7 years for working capital	Must meet SBA size standards, be for-profit, not have internal resources, and be able to demonstrate repayment capability
Microloan Program	Loans are made to nonprofit community lenders who, in turn, make loans to start-up, newly established, or growing businesses—$35,000 maximum, with average loan $10,500, 6-year term— Terms and interest rates vary based on intermediary lender	Start-up, newly established, or growing businesses— criteria and credit requirements determined by local lenders who generally require some type of collateral and personal guarantee

(*Continued*)

Loan Type	Description	Eligibility
Business Physical Disaster Loan	Loans to repair or replace property that suffered physical damage during a disaster—$2 million maximum with 4% or less interest and maturity based on ability to repay	Any business or nonprofit can apply if the area where they are located has been declared a disaster area
CDC (Community Development Company) 504 Program	Long-term financing for economic development within a specified community—Typically, a private investor provides 50%, and CDC provides 40% of the cost and the business applicant provides 10% equity. $2 million at 4% or less for up to 30 years—$1 million maximum for 10 or 20 years with interest pegged to Treasury bonds	Must meet SBA size standards and be located within designated area—Cannot be used, for speculation or investment in rental property or used for working capital or inventory, consolidating or repaying debt or refinancing
Economic Injury Disaster Loans	Loans for small business firms and nonprofit agencies who sustained economic loss but not physical damage during a disaster—$2 million maximum with 4% or less interest and maturity based on ability to repay	Small business, small agricultural cooperatives, and certain nonprofit organizations that can demonstrate substantial economic loss due to a declared physical or an agricultural disaster
Equity Investment (SBIC Program)	The Small Business Investment Company (SBIC) provides equity capital, long term loans and management assistance in a wide variety of fields depending on state and regional needs and resources	Consult SBIC directory to learn about specific opportunities in your geographic area and field of interest
Indian Loans Economic Development	Assists individual Native Americans in obtaining funding from private sources to develop business initiatives in or near federal reservations	You or a family member must be registered in a federally recognized tribe or Alaskan Native village

(Continued)

Loan Type	Description	Eligibility
Military Reservist Economic Injury Disaster Loan Program	Loans for necessary operating expenses small businesses are unable to pay because an essential employee has been "called up" to active duty as a military reservist—$2 million maximum with 4% or less interest and maturity based on ability to repay—intended to only meet necessary obligations as they mature until employee returns	Collateral is required on all loans over $50,000, cannot be used to cover lost income or lost profits or take the place of regular commercial debt
Short–Term Lending Program	One–year renewable line of credit for small businesses involved in transportation-related contracts—interest rate pegged to Wall Street prime	Must be performing federally assisted transportation related project and pay $150 application fee.

Now you probably know more than you ever wanted to know about how the government distributes some of its money through grants. If you want or need to know more, immerse yourself in the resources available at www.Grants .gov or one of the individual departments or agencies.

Final Words About the Political Process

Before we proceed to corporate funding, please allow me one slight, but important, digression because all government grants are highly political, and the more you know about how the system works, the more apt you are to be successful in securing funds. For a brief refresher course in U.S. government and the political process, use your favorite search engine to explore "U.S. political process," visit your closest library or contact an agency that helps immigrants gain their citizenship. Browse a few standard texts, and then pay a visit to the field offices of your elected officials. You are *not* asking for money during this visit (or in any subsequent visit). You are seeking information and establishing relationships. You want to discover how your interests match or don't match your representative's priorities. You want to share information about community and research needs as you perceive them. You want to learn about agencies that reflect your purposes. Most importantly, you want to sign up for mailing lists and email notices about their activities and funding opportunities *before* you read about them in the newspaper. When you return to your office, send the people you met a brief note thanking them for their time and repeating your interest in common topics. Add them to your contact database and don't forget to send them your newsletters and annual reports or invite them to special events. They may not respond or attend your functions, but they will remember your name—and they may even remember to give you a heads-up when new grants are available or legislation is being considered that might affect your work.

ACTIVITIES

1. Contact your school district and city to learn if they have a separate grants office or grants administrator. Make an appointment with that person to learn what grant funds are available for community organizations and what collaborations they are interested in exploring.

2. Learn if your county has a grants office and, if so, what services they offer non-profit organizations.

3. Investigate state departments, agencies, and the governor's office to register for ongoing legislative and funding information and see where funds are currently available.

4. Register for the Arts Council mailing list in your state.

5. Explore www.Grants.gov by:

   • Seeing if there are applicable RFPs at *New Opportunities This Week*

   • Conducting a Basic or Category search for your field of interest

   • Typing a funding number or title you've found in the appropriate box on the Grants Search home page to see if the RFP is applicable. If you are seriously interested in securing government funding, keep looking until you find one or more that matches your project

6. Identify three federal agencies or departments that are relevant to your project and one that is of interest but has no obvious connection. Register for their email lists.

7. Visit field offices of your state and federal elected officials to introduce yourself and your project.

8. Obtain an RFP packet from at least one of the above sources.

Cultivating Corporate and Individual Gifts

We're very effective recyclers; we take the money and give it back.

Paul Newman

My favorite story of resourcefulness in finding a grant comes from a graduate botany student. She was studying in the United States on a student visa from Great Britain and was working part-time to support herself so she wasn't eligible for the grants suggested by her faculty adviser. This didn't stop her from reading the newspaper and professional newsletters, visiting botanical gardens and wildlife preserves in the area, and asking everyone she met if they knew of funding sources. Before long her detective work paid off, and she learned about an association of quail hunters. It turned out that the association owned their own preserve and were more than willing to grant her $500 to catalog the native plants on their property and create a small booklet to use in public information sessions. Because the preserve was not heavily used, she discovered a treasure trove of previously unknown plants—and had material and ideas for years of larger and more prestigious grants and publications.

In this chapter, we'll explore funding sources like that group of quail hunters that are often in our own backyards and are frequently overlooked. Finding them may take some legwork and may use some unorthodox methods of inquiry, but they are often a perfect source for getting a first grant, finding matching funds, or filling a shortfall when a larger grant supplies less than you request. Sometimes, once a relationship has been established, contributions from corporations, individuals, and other groups can become an established part of your yearly income.

Exploring the Corporate World

John Mackey, Co-founder and CEO of Whole Foods Market is widely quoted as saying, "There can be little doubt that a certain amount of corporate philanthropy is simply good business and works for the long-term benefit of the investors." Often corporate leaders are not so open about the connections between their bottom line and their support of community activities, but the reality is they need us as much as we need them. Their purpose is to contribute to a better world, as well as make money for their stockholders. Their employees live in communities that face social problems requiring innovative solutions. Their employees' children go to public and private schools. Their customers look beyond the price tag to consider product quality, effectiveness, and ecological footprints. Their R&D labs are not always able to do the basic or applied research needed to take the next step in their field.

Typically, corporate philanthropy takes five forms: foundation grants, corporate contributions, employee matching gifts, event sponsorships, and in-kind gifts of products or services. Many larger corporations contribute in all five ways, but even the smallest mom-and-pop market will often make a business donation if they are asked.

- **Corporate foundations** abide by the same regulations and are found by the same means as other foundations listed in Chapter 8. You can visit the nearest Foundation Center library to access their corporate directory or subscribe to *Corporate Giving Online* (http://foundationcenter.org/findfunders/fundingsources/cgo.html) for information on corporate donors that support nonprofit organizations and programs through grants as well as in-kind donations of equipment, products, professional services, and volunteers. (Subscriptions for *Corporate Giving Online* are priced from $59.95 a month.)

    Another option is to look for specialized search engines or build your own database from information you find in professional journals, TV ads, newspaper stories and ads, billboards, special event programs, etc. For example, Teachers Count (www.teacherscount.org) provides a variety of resources for classroom teachers including sources of grants for both professional development and classroom projects.

Corporations like publicity so you'll find their names almost everyplace you look. Corporations are also technologically savvy, so when you have a handful of likely prospects, enter the company name followed by "foundation" in your favorite search engine and see what you can find. When I did this on a random collection of two dozen names from a day's collection, all of the corporations had foundations or a charitable giving program of some kind. Of course, not all of them will provide grants that are relevant to your current needs, but since I chose national chains with products like fast food, office supplies, pharmacy, clothing, technology, y all give money to groups in my t step in the sorting process.

from corporate foundations and ou may find them listed under the lations, community relations, comity, social investments, community t the process becomes very similar undation. They will have printed process or contact person. Follow le and if there is a match between

made at a local level rather than a he most direct route is through the ir name through the Chamber of ectly. Once you have a name, make imes managers have a discretionary es they are the gatekeepers to larger ommittees play a part in deciding nded. Funding priorities vary from business to business, and often change as management changes. In any event, you need to know the situation at the specific store, plant, distribution facility, or branch office in your community.

For example, there are eight Target stores within a ten-mile radius of my office in suburban Los Angeles. They each have a different "signature" project. This year, one sponsored back-to-school shopping trips for low-income children, another provided new clothing and shoes for a hospital auxiliary to give rape survivors, a third sponsored a Dress-for-Success day

---

Union West Regional
01/27/2022 3:48:20 PM   704-283-8184

Overdue fines are 25¢ per day and the maximum fine per item is $10.00.

Title: Grant writing demystified /
Item ID: 8710910004190005
Due: 02/17/2022

Want to pick up your hold after hours? Ask about our Book Lockers!

with donated wardrobes, free haircuts, and job search skills for homeless shelter residents. The others donated backpacks for kindergarten children, supplied equipment for an informal neighborhood sports program, sponsored families for holidays, and collected staples for food banks. They all donated gift cards and baskets for raffles, bought program ads and golf tournament sponsorships, and otherwise supported myriad local groups. Some donations were probably responses to a form letter, but my conversations with managers leads me to believe the more substantial contributions come as a result of a face-to-face request that made the connection between the group asking for help and the interests and needs of the stores' employees and customers. The same process works with vendors and people who supply your agency, school, hospital, or other place of employment, although this may take a few more steps to find someone in management.

- **Employee matching gifts** are most frequently associated with companies matching the amount their employees give to United Way, college alumni funds, or well-known health charities like the American Cancer Society, but many companies will also match funds for smaller groups so it doesn't hurt to ask someone in human resources. If they do, you have three routes to explore. One is to hold a mini-campaign among their employees that is tied to a special event; the second is to provide information for in-house newsletters and posters and donation envelopes for a small display in the human resources office; and the third is to use your internal communication systems to identify spouses and current supporters who work for the targeted firms. Employee gifts are often small, but they add up and often become a reliable and steady proportion of an annual fundraising campaign. They can also be a source of funds when a grant requires matching funds on your part.

- **Event sponsorships** are traditional ways to secure funds from banks, car dealerships, construction companies, and other high-visibility local firms for direct fundraising activities like golf tournaments, recognition banquets, walkathons, and big ticket auctions. Personal contact is the key ingredient when looking for an event sponsorship. Some companies will only give money for special events to an organization on the recommendation of an employee in a management position. You may get door prizes or items for goodie bags from a well-written letter, but if you want a $5,000 sponsorship for a fashion show or a cruise for a raffle prize, you need to know somebody who knows somebody who can authorize that kind of contribution with a handshake. This isn't impossible if you do several brainstorming sessions with the people you know and believe in the six degrees of separation concept. Consider vendors and others who have a vested interest in your project—and go in pairs if you're afraid of asking in person. Remember, "people give to people" so establish a relationship well before you ask for a donation. Finally, present your request as an opportunity for community service rather than as a plea for help. Make the transaction a win-win situation—and you can return next year.

One caveat—do *not* expect to receive event sponsorships from a foundation unless they specifically include them in their guidelines. Most foundations clearly exclude all special events from projects they fund. Many even include a list of activities they will not consider—but they report they still receive requests. "But you said no golf tournaments or fashion shows, and this is a bike-a-thon" is not a justification. Be warned that asking for something that is remotely connected to an item on the exclusion list is the kiss of death to any future request to that foundation. Even if your next request is for a project that falls within their guidelines, their records will show you didn't read the directions once in the distant past and your current application will be quickly rejected without a second thought.

- **In-kind gifts of products and services** are another traditional form corporate contributions can take. A nursery donates tomato plants for an elementary school class project, a carpet store installs flooring in a make-over house for Christmas in April, a bank donates desks and chairs when it closes a branch, or a CPA firm offers a junior associate at a discounted price for your required audit. A personal face-to-face request works best for local items you discover through informal means but a letter to larger regional or national companies works for ongoing needs like personal care items for a residential program or toys for an annual holiday drive. If you love the thrill of yard sales and finding a good bargain, there are regional and national groups that exist solely to make matches between companies and nonprofit groups. Gifts in Kind International (www.giftsinkind.org) and the National Assoiation for the Exchange of Industrial Resources (www.naeir.org) have contracts with major corporations like IBM, Microsoft, Mattel, Avon, Gillette, Office Depot, and Radio Shack to collect and distribute new, overstock inventory. Others like Freecycle (www.freecycle.org) are regional volunteer efforts. Some local and regional distribution centers specialize in food products, others in furniture and office supplies, and others in recycled technology. None can supply all of your needs immediately since their stock varies greatly and merchandise is usually distributed on a first-come, first-served basis.

In-kind services are an often overlooked contribution corporations can make as part of a required match for a grant or as a way for a small agency to find relief for their operating budget. You can apply for consultant services for staff or board training, help with personnel policies, legal advice, and financial or technology support. Some companies allow employees to volunteer on company time for a local charity of their own choosing for a specified amount of time each month, and a few companies follow up with a small contribution to each organization where an employee volunteers.

One of the best ways to find in-kind donations is to poll friends, relatives, co-workers, and their spouses. A large preschool program received three pallets of discontinued office supplies that included gold paper clips and enough wastebaskets to supply the schools where they were housed because a teacher's husband saw them being loaded and asked if they could be delivered to his wife's preschool instead of the recycling center. A single phone call assured him they would be delivered in an hour. Another organization received pro-bono legal advice in setting up their 501(c)(3) corporation from a lawyer the secretary of the board met at a block party.

Corporate Commonalities

Regardless of whether funds come from the corporate foundation or one of the other avenues, there are several factors all corporate contributions share. Here are a few I've discovered.

- Most grant recipients are located within a 50-mile radius of the corporate office, manufacturing facility, retail outlet, or other place of the grantmaker's business. Don't ask Union Pacific for a grant unless you're located near one of their railroads. Most foundation guidelines mention geographic restrictions, but corporate giving programs often assume you know that.

- While most grants are made to reflect the company's overall purpose, don't assume they all are. For example, Abbott Laboratories funds pharmaceutical research and donates nutritional products, but the company also supports numerous programs for children affected by HIV/AIDS and has an extensive employee volunteer program. Do an online search before you query.

- Businesses like to see their money at work so make sure your project is visible and the donors are acknowledged appropriately. Although corporations cannot benefit directly from their gift to a nonprofit agency or research facility, they do appreciate the goodwill generated by public announcements of their generosity. Take care to publicize their grant or other contribution in both public and private ways, but be sensitive to what is meaningful to them. Sometimes pictures for their in-house newsletter are more appropriate than a photo of three people in suits holding a giant check in the local newspaper. Sometimes they may wish to remain anonymous, and sometimes they'd like a room in a new building or a summer jazz camp named after them. It's a truism that the closer the match of the thank-you to what is appreciated in the corporate culture, the more likely you will continue to receive support from that source.

Consider the Source

There is one important consideration when accepting funds from a corporate sponsor and that is guilt by association. I have a hunch more people recognize a corporation's logo and brand name faster and more accurately than they recognize yours so be careful. Make sure the company image supports your mission. Teachers accepting classroom materials, lesson plans, videos, and other support from corporations need to be especially careful of the implicit as well as explicit messages being taught. For example, Nike has an exciting exercise program for preschool children who do not have access to outside play space, but you may not want to imply Nike shoes are the best brand to buy. Similarly, if you provide support services to recovering alcoholics, you probably do not want your name seen next to Budweiser or Coors, even though both corporations are generous supporters of community projects. Susan G. Komen Race for the Cure discovered the negative effects of a mismatch when public outcry derailed their partnership with KFC. Enough people made a negative connection between fried food and cancer to cause a dent in income for both groups. On the other hand, the partnership between Home Depot and Habitat for Humanity works because both are interested in providing safe, comfortable, functional housing. Home Depot's involvement with KaBOOM! community playgrounds also works because local employees volunteer time, energy, and tools to erect play structures in parks in their community as a way of working side by side with and saying thank you to people who patronize their stores.

Focus Locally

Once again, if you are new at raising funds from corporations, I suggest you start at the local end of the spectrum and work your way up. Read the business section of the local newspaper for announcements of grand openings and expansion plans. Collect lists of the largest employers in all the communities within a 50-mile radius of your program activities. Get to know the managers of several banks and chain stores in your area. Find out who the community representatives for local utilities are. Cultivate a connection between their mission and your dream. Marketing experts tell us a minimum of seven repetitions are necessary before someone remembers the name of a company, so develop a least a half-dozen ways to interact with your prospects before you ask for money.

- Send an email or brief note—good to meet you at ____," "congratulations on ____," or "as a company that manufactures/sells X, you might be interested in the Y services our agency provides."
- Arrange a brief visit (10 or 15 minutes maximum) at their place of visit or your agency or school.
- Invite them to a free activity scheduled for the near future.
- Say hi when you visit their store.
- Send more notes, sometimes with a clipping of mutual interest.
- Ask board members and program participants to join you in patronizing their business and mentioning your programs.
- Ask for advice on something that doesn't cost money.
- Refer a potential customer or client—and remind that person to mention the source of the referral.

Don't be obsequious or cloying with your attention. Just be persistent, creative, and genuine. Consider the time these activities take as community education, donor cultivation, marketing, word-of-mouth advertising, whatever makes it easier for you. If there's no real connection, cut your losses and continue with other prospects but don't burn your bridges. If you develop a mutually beneficial relationship, corporations can be your best friends.

Other Sources of Funds

You know by now that I follow my grandmother's advice to not put all my eggs in one basket. While I'm busy researching and writing grant proposals—and waiting to hear the results—I'm also investigating other sources of funds like corporate contributions. Here are six more that might be applicable for your search:

1. Individuals
2. Federated giving groups
3. Civic organizations
4. Giving circles
5. Special interest clubs
6. Online donation

The Power of One

Three times as much money is contributed to charitable causes each year by individuals than by corporations and foundations combined. According to Giving USA, individual giving in 2008 was estimated to be over $229 billion or over 75 percent of total donations. While about half of that goes to religious congregations, educational institutions, family foundations, and health organizations, over $56 billion is left for individual gifts for other charities. That's a lot of money to ignore, so let's look at how someone who writes grant proposals relates to this source of funding.

You've read repeatedly in this and previous chapters about the importance of cultivating personal relationships with members of family foundations and with corporate personnel. The same principles and approaches work with individuals. While it may seem like a good idea to write a letter to the latest lottery winner or hottest rock star asking for funds to help runaway teens or find a cure for asthma, don't. The larger the sum of money you want, the more important the relationship between the donor and the person or group receiving the money is. Take time to find someone who already knows the individual you want to approach, ask for an introduction, cultivate the relationship, and then use a written proposal to reinforce verbal conversations and make implicit agreements explicit. This written document needs to be as carefully crafted as all the other grant proposals you write, but it needs to be laced with specific, personal details that tap into the donor's motivation for giving.

Much noise is made about the tax benefits of giving to charitable causes. While this is an important consideration for some people, it is not the primary motivation for most of us. People give to museums, sexual assault programs, agricultural research, and all of the other causes we represent for five basic reasons:

- **They have a personal experience with the value of your work or cause**. Someone's parent died of complications from diabetes so the person has a vested interest in research, or new forms of treatment, or hospice care, or new prosthetic development, or Meals on Wheels, or some other aspect of living and dying with the disease. Listen carefully and you'll find the connections.

- **They want to be part of something larger than themselves.** Everyone feels discouraged at times when the challenges they face personally or in their communities seem overwhelming. You know you can't combat gang violence single-handedly but you feel better about yourself when you give a contribution to Home Boys Industries or support a tattoo removal program. You know your solos in the shower won't win any prizes, but you can contribute to the symphony or local music school or junior high jazz band so that others can enjoy music of the ages.

- **People want to leave a legacy.** While this is similar to the first two motivations, leaving a legacy implies having particular interests or skills someone wants to leave for future generations. The author leaves her notebooks to a library in hopes that future students will remember her through her scribblings. A couple designate funds to an animal shelter to protect pets that mean so much to their family. An orange grove becomes a conservancy to maintain a slice of history.

- **People give from feelings of gratitude.** People remember the swimming lessons at the Y, the life-changing words of a particular teacher, and excitement when their grandfather took them to the observatory for their first time—and they want to say thank you.

- **People give from feelings of guilt.** When we see someone who is less fortunate than we are, we have a choice between sharing our resources from a posture of gratitude or guilt. Guilt is often the stronger of the two emotions—and many appeal letters are written to trigger this motivation. It works, and it's effective for many groups as seen in the large amount of direct mail I receive with heart-wrenching pictures and stories.

When you are speaking to potential donors, look for which motivations are likely to be strongest and support those emotional decisions. This doesn't mean being blatant about saying, "Because you sister died of breast cancer, and you feel guilty because you didn't, you need to give to cancer research." It simply means being sensitive to the mix of reasons people might choose to support your project. It also means that after some general conversation about mutual interests you include phrases like:

- "Because we know attending the high school musicals is so important to you, we want to give you an opportunity to help us refurbish the sound system at Anytown High School."
- "I was excited to learn about your collection of rare butterflies and hope you might have an interest in exploring ways we might work together on a project the Institute is considering in the Amazon."
- "As the owner of a thriving nursery business, I know you appreciate the challenges of attracting key people for critical positions. As we seek funds for the new program in plant genetics, we would like to include Petersen's Plant Patio in the list of local supporters who will provide matching funds for the director's salary for the first year."

These are crude sketches, but you get the idea of interweaving a person's known interest and possible motivation with a request for support.

The Power of Association

In 1887, a priest, two ministers and a rabbi joined together to raise $21,700 for 22 agencies in Denver. Maybe they were tired of having to say no to countless good people asking for help. Maybe they recognized the value of a coordinated appeal. Whatever the reason for their action, these four men are credited with establishing the precursor to Community Chests, which later became United Way. For over a century, individuals and local business firms were encouraged to "Give once and you give to all." As special interest groups proliferated and began seeking funds independently, United Ways began to lose some of their appeal and effectiveness, but don't write them off as obsolete. In more and more communities, United Way acts like a catalyst for change by funding initiatives that address emerging problems rather than being a conduit for funds for established agencies. It's important to check out the United Way in your area to see what they are doing. You may discover, as I did, that they are a treasure trove of valuable information on community needs and resources and have more available funding than I expected.

The concept of sharing fundraising tasks and determining its distribution is not limited to United Way, however. The United Jewish Appeal, the Jewish

Federation of North America, the United Negro College Fund, United Catholic Charities, and the Combined Federal Campaign are all alive and well. In some senses, community foundations are essentially a variation on the theme because smaller foundations (rather than individuals) contribute to a larger pool where their money can be managed, invested, and distributed by another entity.

Grant makers are also banding together to form affinity groups like the Women's Funding Network, Funders Concerned about AIDS, the Association of Small Foundations and Hispanics in Philanthropy. As an article by Marc Green for the Grantsmanship Center points out, however, affiliations are organized for the benefit of grant makers not grant seekers. While they may make a database of their members public as a resource for potential funding sources, their primary benefit isn't money but resource materials, data, and ideas. Green cites the example of Grantmakers in Aging (www.giaging.org) that puts out a handbook that contains capsule descriptions of successfully funded programs in various parts of the country.

Another Idea Reborn

To return to sources of funds, **giving clubs** and **giving circles** are a combination of an old idea and a relatively new phenomenon. Informal associations called giving circles were popular means of supporting widows, orphans, and other neighbors down on their luck in ethnic communities in the early 20th century. Many disbanded as neighborhoods changed, and others consolidated to form the federations mentioned previously. At the same time, investment clubs were formed to protect people's investments. As financial institutions proliferated and became more dependable, investment clubs changed focus to become educational tools to help women and others with limited financial experience learn about and manage monetary investments. Each person in a group of six to eight people contributes a minimum amount each month, which is pooled and invested in stocks and bonds chosen by the group as a whole. The same idea works today with social investments. The new giving clubs are small cohorts of friends, neighbors, or business associates who pool their contributions, research local needs, and then "invest" the entire amount in donations to local charities according to a majority decision. According to an American Express charitable gift survey in 2007, giving circle members are more likely than other donors to give to organizations serving women and girls, ethnic and minority groups, and for arts, culture, and ethnic awareness and are less likely to give to federated funds like the United Way or to religious organizations. Membership and recipients may vary from year to year because they are generally formed by word of mouth and subsequent organization tends to be relatively informal. Communication is handled online or over coffee or drinks in someone's home. As you can imagine, there is no central directory and online searches are not very productive in locating giving circles or social investment clubs. Bloggers seem to know about them and sometimes you run across a reference on someone's Facebook. I have no good advice on how to find one in your area, except to keep your ears open and your antenna alert because you may find a private fund few people know about.

Online Possibilities

Creativity is rampant on the Internet, and I'm sure there will be dozens of new options every year. The first and simplest step is to make sure your web site is configured to accept donations online. Change the appeal frequently, add a seasonal wish list, or request matching funds for a new project. Three other programs or ideas I know that have been successfully used in 2010 are:

- **Facebook "Causes"**—www.facebook.com—One way to celebrate the organization's anniversary, launch a new program, or honor a well-known volunteer or board member is to hold a time-limited drive on the agency's or person's Facebook. Encourage people to send a child to camp, choose and buy a chair for the new performance hall, or do any one of the designated campaigns you now do by word-of-mouth and mail campaigns. The keys are to be specific and to set a time limit.

- **Kickstarter**—www.kickstarter.com—If you're an artist, musician, solo researcher, or grassroots group not incorporated as a 501(c)(3) organization, consider one of the online services like Kickstarter to solicit funds for individual projects directly. You simply describe your activities, set a financial goal and campaign time frame, and provide incentives for pledges. Requests range from $1,500 for supplies not included in an art residency grant to $5,000 to cover grain elevators with murals to $80,000 for a benefit concert. Time parameters range from 30 to 90 days. If the monetary goal is not reached within the prescribed time, pledges are not cashed out and the project is not funded. On the other hand, if the goal is reached within the time frame, additional pledges can be made and will be added to the total. Kickstarter charges 5 percent of the amount pledged to cover administrative costs.

- **Donors Choose**—www.donorschoose.org—If you're a classroom teacher, librarian, school counselor, or other frontline school staff member and need specific materials for a project, check out this easy-to-use service. You send a picture, description of your situation, and a detailed list of the specific supplies you need. Donors make a credit card "purchase" just like shopping online. Donors Choose staff purchase requested items and mail them to your school. Your students send thank-you notes and videos, which are posted with your progress report. The guidelines recommend projects costing under $400 have the best chance of being funded, but a request for a $1,000 timpani from a Connecticut school in a high-poverty area had raised $850 within five months and had a month to go in their campaign. Having a compelling story and a tangible result are keys to success in this venue just as they are with more traditional funding sources. The site also lists other corporate and foundation funding opportunities for classroom teachers by state.

First, Last, and Foremost, Concentrate on One-on-One Networking

You know by now that I'm convinced the most effective route to obtaining grants from corporations, local groups, and individuals is through personal contact. I'm also convinced that the most efficient and effective method of establishing that contact is through networking. To paraphrase the epigram from Chapter 2 the best way to establish good contacts is to make lots of contacts. My children and husband fuss with me because I speak to everyone I meet no matter where I am: church, grocery store, restaurant, concert, or town hall meeting. It pays off however, when I need an introduction to a person, business, or other resource to take an ordinary grant request to a stellar proposal. I encourage you to establish a similar habit.

ACTIVITIES

1. Identify three or more corporate foundations or giving programs that might fund your project.

2. Interview a retail store manager or vendor to learn how his/her corporation funds community activities.

3. Identify three or more sources of in-kind donations, and secure at least one product or service donation.

4. List corporations you would not accept funds from for ethical or conflict of interest reasons.

5. Choose at least six forms of cultivating a prospective donor and implement two or more.

6. Imagine a person who might want to make a sizeable contribution to your project and write the first few sentences you might say to introduce your request for a donation.

7. Browse online funding sites and sketch a presentation you might make for an element of your project.

chapter 11

Reading Guidelines and RFPs

> *Lions and tigers and bears! Oh my!*
>
> Judy Garland as Dorothy in The Wizard of Oz

Once you've identified several funding sources that look like they might fund your project, it's time to do some detective work to determine how close the match really is. The first step in this part of the process is to carefully read the material you've collected already to see what you know and what gaps are left to fill. To avoid the dead end we encountered with the federal posting for migratory bird research in Chapter 9, I've developed a routine as I scan announcements and RFPs.

1. **Check to make sure you are eligible.** Some foundations now offer a short online survey to determine eligibility. Often there are geographic restrictions. Sometimes applications are accepted by invitation only or funds are reserved for a continuation of a specific project. Sometimes grants require collaboration with a partner you don't have. If you're not eligible, record the name of the foundation or federal grant category in a special computer file labeled "Dead Ends" or "Inappropriate Funding Sources" with a dated note about why it wasn't a match. Later, when a board member sees a newspaper article about another agency receiving an astronomical grant and suggests you apply to the same funding source, this is the first file to check. It's faster and easier than repeating the original search, and

it provides an accurate address to check to see if their funding guidelines have changed. If you were ineligible for a reason that can be changed like finding a suitable collaborative partner or obtaining your 501(c)(3) designation, you now have a head start locating funding sources when the situation changes.

2. **Check the deadline and your calendar.** Unless this is a renewal application or you've written a proposal for a similar project that has been rejected, give yourself at least a month to prepare a letter of intent (LOI) or two months for a full proposal. If there is less time than that, place the prospect on the calendar for next year.

3. **Now focus on four of the five W's and H taught in journalism school—Who, What, When, Where and How.** I leave out "why" because why questions speak to motivation, and no one can answer them except the person who asked them. You won't know why Foundation X wants the program description before the community assessment and why Foundation Y wants the order reversed. You will have no idea why the government wants much of the information they ask for but you need to provide it anyway. Ultimately, you won't know why your proposal was or wasn't funded, so you can save yourself a lot of grief by simply omitting why questions from your vocabulary.

Focusing on the third element above, five questions are going to be more than enough because you want to ask the same questions in different ways and hear the answers so often they become almost automatic. You want to know as much as you can about the funder because you want to match your proposal to what they want to fund as closely as possible. You want to pick up the cadence of their writing, the themes that are important, the unspoken culture of the foundation or government agency. You want to use your intuition, as well as your critical thinking skills. When you start writing, you want to leave your world and climb inside the world of the funder.

Here are a few questions to get started, but feel free to add your own.

- **Who** can apply for funds? Who is not eligible? Who has received money in the past? Who will review the application? Who makes the final decision?

- **What** is the range of the grant awards? What activities does the foundation fund? What information do they want about the agency? What information do they want about the project? What attachments are required? What are the scoring criteria? What reports are required?

- **When** is the submission deadline? When are grant decisions made? When will the money be available?

- **Where** is the foundation located? Where do they fund projects? Where do I go to get more information?

- **How** do I submit a proposal—online or by mail? How will applications be judged? How much money is available? How many grants are funded each year?

Organizing Information So You Can Find It

To make the process easier and to keep track of the information, I complete a form like the Funding Opportunity Fact Sheet as I answer the questions. This is my own creation, but there are similar forms available to download for free from both the Grantsmanship and Foundation Centers (www.tgci.com and www.foundationcenter.org).

FUNDING OPPORTUNITY FACT SHEET	
Title	
Funding Source	
Award Amount	
Number of Awards	
Required Match	
Funding Duration	
Deadline	Letter of Intent: Full Proposal
Submission Method	Mailed Packet or Online
Overview	
Project Types	
Funding Priorities	
Funding Exclusions	
Critical Elements	
Impact to Agency	
Contact	Guidelines at:
	Submit to:
	Program Officer:
	Email: Phone: Fax:
Other Information	

Now we'll explore how the chart would look after reading this fictional notice from a funding newsletter:

Funding from the Amelia Langdon Webb Foundation is currently available to support direct costs for catalogues and other publications accompanying contemporary art exhibitions and projects, especially those supporting emerging and under-recognized artists and produced by smaller organizations outside the nation's cultural centers. Limited funds are also available for publications related to the grantee organization and its programs or collections. The foundation does not provide grants for individuals, general operating expenses, capital campaigns, endowment funds, or projects supporting the work of deceased artists and prefers one-time special projects that are originated by the applying organization. Requests for projects that take place within a year of the request will be given priority consideration. Applicant organizations must have current tax-exempt status under the Internal Revenue Code. Grant amounts typically range from $5,000 to $20,000. Proposals for funding are reviewed semi-annually, in the spring and fall. Letters of Inquiry are required before submission of a full proposal and are accepted throughout the year for preliminary review but must be received by March 15 for the spring funding cycle and by August 15 for the fall funding cycle.

Grant link: http://www.alwfoundation.com/applicationguidelines.html

FUNDING OPPORTUNITY FACT SHEET

Title	Art Exhibit Catalogs & Publications
Funding Source	Amelia Langdon Webb Foundation
Award Amount	$5,000 to $20,000
Number of Awards	
Required Match	
Funding Duration	
Deadline	Letter of Intent: first step foundation 3–15 (our deadline 2–15) and foundation 8–15 (ours 7–15) Full Proposal if LOI approved
Submission Method	Mailed Packet
Overview	Direct costs for publications for contemporary art exhibits and projects
Project Types	Publications for specific art exhibits Publications related to grantee organization and its programs
Funding Priorities	Emerging and under–recognized artists smaller organizations outside recognized cultural centers one-time projects originated by applicant event held within a year of request
Funding Exclusions	Individuals, general operating expenses, capital campaigns, endowment funds, work of deceased artists
Critical Elements	Must have background work started with commitment from an artist and reserved space
Impact to Agency	
Contact	Guidelines at: http://www.alwfoundation.com/applicationguidelines.html Submit to: Program Officer: Email: Phone: Fax:
Other Information	

Before we take the next step of going to the web site to read the guidelines, let me add a few notes about how I read between the lines of even a seemingly simple notice.

Starting with the eligibility, deadlines, and other logistical concerns, I notice:

- **Current tax-exempt status** means you must have that important 501(c)(3) letter from the IRS.

- The grant range of **$5,000 to $20,000** is typical for foundations named after an individual. You'll want to ask for their Annual Report or check out their 990 form at The Foundation Center (www.foundationcenter. org) or GuideStar (www.guidestar.org) to find out how many grants they make each year and what the average amount is. I've known some foundations that make one large award and the rest at the lower end of the scale. In that case, asking for $15,000 will get you nowhere. For now, however, simply note the range, start a wish list, and get some preliminary price quotes from local printers.

- Like many foundations, the Amelia Langdon Webb Foundation, accepts letters of intent (LOIs) throughout the year and reviews proposals at selected times (**semi-annually in the spring and fall**). The important deadlines are **March 15 and August 15** because they are cut-off dates for LOIs and give you a hint of when funding decisions are made. You'll notice I put earlier dates in parenthesis after the deadlines in the chart. That's because you'll want your letter to arrive in the middle of the submissions and not at the beginning or the end. Foundation program staff tend to read submissions as they come in and separate them into piles: definite yes, definite no, and maybe. As the deadline approaches, they will be reading applications from procrastinators who wait until the last minute, as well as rereading those in the maybe pile, which psychologically doubles the competition.

I pay special attention to the funders' description of what they are looking for. Each word has been chosen carefully even though it may seem generic or ambiguous. If you are unsure if your idea fits their guidelines, ask a program officer when you call or email.

- **Direct costs for catalogues and other publications** means printing, binding, photography, copy writing, and other tangible costs involved in producing printed documents. It does not mean refreshments for a reception, travel expenses for the illustrator, or installation costs for an exhibit.

- The catalogues and publications must **focus on a contemporary art exhibition or project** and can't be used for a CD of a drumming group, an exhibit of Old Masters, or a display of Mayan artifacts. Funds could provide handouts for a family program to accompany the exhibit or worksheets for student tours, however, and might be broad enough to cover study materials for volunteer docents or audio recordings. Ask when you speak to the program officer.

- **Emerging and under-recognized artists** is a broad field. To state the obvious, to meet this criteria means you have already chosen the artist or artists for the exhibit and have extensive biographical information on emerging trends in the field, the importance of their work, and their limited exposure. "Contemporary" means they are probably living or have only recently died. Reading further you know the person must be living because the notice specifically excludes the work of deceased artists. An explicit message is that the closer you can tie the chosen artists to your local community and/or the mission and ongoing focus of your agency, the stronger your proposal will be.

- The phrase **smaller organizations outside the nation's cultural centers** makes me beam with joy. I grew up in a small South Dakota college town and learned to appreciate attention paid to those of us outside the usual spotlight. As a current resident of the Southern California sprawl known as the Inland Empire, I would focus on these words to show that people in our area are hesitant to travel to Los Angles or San Diego to view works of a local son or daughter who has moved to the big city.

- **Limited funds are available** opens the door for investigation with the program officer. Have one or two projects in mind before you call so when he or she asks what you have in mind, you have a ready answer.

I pay even more attention to what the foundation does *not* provide grants for. This list is typical for most foundations.

- **Individuals**, even artists and other who have formed a single-person non-profit are generally excluded from grants. You'll note this foundation funds publications *about* the work but does not include stipends for artists to attend the exhibit or give related workshops or master classes. Those funds will need to come from another source.

- **General operating expenses** are also the agency's responsibility, although this is an area to watch. As the economic situation has changed, more and more funders are allowing related operating expenses to be included in the grant budget. I still find it easier to include a percentage of the curator, publicist, and receptionist salaries as matching or in-kind funds rather than asking for them as direct funds, even if these people will be doing extra work to implement the project

- Even if this will be the first exhibit in a new wing to your existing building, don't even try to link this request to your **capital campaign**. Focus on what Amelia Langdon Webb and her descendants want the money to fund, i.e., publications.

- Again, an **endowment fund** to support other emerging and under-recognized artists is a worthy cause, but don't consider asking this foundation for help in establishing or adding to yours. They are *not* interested.

Finally, when the guidelines state a preference—**prefers one-time special projects that are originated by the applying organization . . . that take place within one year of the request**—pay attention. In this day of extreme competition when even the smallest foundations receive eight to ten times more requests than they can fund, consider this a requirement and not a request. Also give credence to each word and phrase. "One-time," "special project," "originated by applying organization"—when taken as a group—suggest a retrospective of a local ceramicist's work on his 60th birthday, a collection of art quilts to commemorate the town's 100th anniversary, or an exhibit of interpretations of last year's forest fires by local artists in several mediums.

Dealing with Jargon

In spite of efforts to simplify the language and application process, government RFPs are still burdened with bureaucratic gobbledy-gook. Jake and Isaac Seliger (www.seliger.com) have a great time collecting and playing with obtuse questions, repetitive instructions, and contradictory pronouncements. There is really no way to deal with over-stuffed sentences except to laugh at them and then use common sense in translating them. Some grant professionals keep a file of the most convoluted verbiage they find to review on days when the latest RFP seems impossible to decipher. I don't do that but I do have a few suggestions on how to deal with jargon, however.

- Know your field. If you read professional journals, attend symposiums, and otherwise keep abreast of trends in your profession, you'll recognize much of the jargon as current buzzwords.

- Attend any and all bidders' conferences, funders' forums, and workshops sponsored by the Association of Fundraising Professionals (AFP) and similar groups. Not only will new terms be defined and illustrated, but you will have the opportunity to ask questions if you don't understand. As a bonus, meet the presenter to take that important first step in building a relationship where you can ask for further assistance and clarification when you need it.

- Add really puzzling queries to your list of topics for a conversation with the program officer of the relevant funding source.

Mining for Additional Information

As mentioned in Chapter 9 on finding government funds, most of the information you need to apply for a grant is online. The same is true for most foundations. This doesn't mean you will understand everything you read or have all of your questions answered, but it does mean you have more research to do before you start writing. At a minimum, you'll want to locate the complete funding guidelines, all of the application forms, and information about past recipients of grants. You'll also want to gather as much information as you can about the "culture" of the funding source by obtaining their annual reports, scanning newspaper accounts of their activities, checking their 990 tax reports, and learning who is on their board of directors or review panels. Each piece of information paints a clearer picture of who you are entering into a relationship with—and makes writing the proposal, negotiating the terms of the contract, and meeting their expectations for program implementation that much easier.

Important documents to find and study are sample proposals that have been successful for each funding source you select. I have purposely chosen not to include any in this book for several reasons.

- The temptation to plagiarize is almost overwhelming, especially if this is your first proposal or you're on a tight deadline. Copying is not only unethical, but it will be discovered.

- In spite of a trend to standardize application forms and procedures, all funders retain unique aspects that you need to notice. This is particularly true if you have not applied for funds from them before.

- A sample LOI or funding narrative I created for this book would only be a demonstration of my skill (or lack thereof) and of little value to you. I think you'll have a much better learning experience from skimming actual samples you've discovered for yourself.

- Finally, sample proposals are amazingly easy to locate. Program officers of many foundations and most government agencies will email you one if you ask—and asking is a good excuse to call or email them as an introduction to other questions you may have. If the grant maker balks, ask a colleague or one of the previously funded agencies for a copy of one of their successful ones. Although this would be viewed as competition in the business world, sharing is expected in the nonprofit sector—and your projects will be different anyway. Because samples are a frequent freebie on grant writing blogs and consultants' web sites, you can also simply search "sample grant narratives" on the Internet. You'll literally find millions.

Having listed all my objections, I repeat my advice to find and read samples of good proposals to absorb the flow and format of the genre. Just as poets fill their shelves with books of poetry and novelists carry fiction paperbacks everywhere they go, those of us who write grants need to be steeped in our particular craft. Watch the pacing. See how phrases are repeated and changed. Check to see how jargon is translated into words you understand. Look for concepts that are important to particular funders. Notice how each section is self-contained yet bridges to another one. We'll touch on more of these writing techniques in Chapter 12 when we focus on writing the narrative, so for now, concentrate on soaking up the intangible "culture" of the particular foundation or government agency you are researching.

Once you've located materials about several funding sources, study them in detail. Make hard copies of everything you find online or borrow. Highlight and underline. Circle words you don't understand. Jot down questions. While it is two or three times more important to read every word in the foundation guidelines and the government RFP, it's also critical to pay close attention to other documents like the annual report, list of recent grants, members on the board and/or review team, and how they are presented in the media. Sift and sort and ponder all the information you can find about the funder and the application process—and then contact the person listed in the announcement and ask your questions.

Setting Priorities

While multitasking is the norm when preparing for writing proposals, it's important to prioritize the order and timing of writing and submitting applications so you can focus on one at a time. You know how easy it is to call one of your children by a sibling's name when you're in a rush. And you know how furious they are when you do so. Grant makers are even less forgiving. Don't run the risk of making a simple mistake like leaving the wrong initials in a copied paragraph or mixing up project budgets. Don't laugh. Reviewers swear it happens.

I use two tools to help me analyze, prioritize, and organize funding opportunities. The first is the analysis chart that collects the answers to my "four W and an H" questions. I fill one out for each foundation or government RFP that looks feasible and place one copy in that particular folder to use when I'm ready to work on that proposal and one copy in a three-ring binder for easier access before then. Yes, there will be holes at this point, but you know you'll fill them eventually as the process continues.

Analysis of Potential Funding Opportunity	
Title	
Funding Source	
Award Amount	
Number of Awards	
Required Match	
Funding Duration	
Deadline	Letter of Intent Full Proposal
Alignment with Mission	
Alignment with Long- and Short-Term Goals	
Key Staff to Implement Project	
Potential Partners	
Feasibility Considerations	
Additional Information Needed	
Decisions to Be Made	

Creating a Grants Calendar

The second document is a calendar of due dates, requests submitted, rejections, and awards. It can be a simple listing of grant maker, amount to request, and deadline or can be a more complicated form created on Excel for easy sorting. Because many foundations accept LOIs throughout the year, I often arrange items in a calendar by criteria other than deadline dates so I can find a particular funding source or write a report for the board on the status of grants. I also cut and paste sometimes to pull out those that I think have the best chance for success, are easy to prepare, or match a particular project that is ready to go rather than give the board the whole laundry list to consider.

Here is a simple chart that shows how a small fictional art museum might schedule their grant requests.

Grant Maker	Amount to Request	Deadline
First Bank of North Hills	$2,500	Open
Foothill Power and Light	$2,500	Quarterly
Brown County Art Alliance	$5,000	Feb 8, 2011
National Society of Art Lovers	$5,000	May 15, 2011
Kathleen Wagner Family Foundation	$10,000	June 15, 2011
Studebaker Family Trust	$15,000	June 30, 2011
The Evergreen Trust	$25,000	July 15, 2011

A more elaborate form I might use to educate and report to the board is the Grants Calendar.

Grants Calendar

Deadline	Funding Source	Focus	$ Range	Submission Method	Comments	Status

Filled in, it might look something like the second example.

Deadlines	Funding Source	Focus	$ Range	Submission Method	Comments	Status
Year-round funding	**Ahmanson Foundation** 9215 Wilshire Blvd. Beverly Hills 90210 www.theahmanson foundation.org (310) 278-0770	4 areas including arts & humanities Los Angeles County Construction, renovation technology, equipment, infrastructure	$10,000 – $30,000 One year funding	Letter of inquiry mailed	Likes matching grants	Applied 2-1-10 $26,500 science lab upgrades pending
Board reviews and grants made in April & Aug	**Rose Hills Foundation** www.rosehills foundation.org 444 South Flower St. #1450 Los Angeles 90071 (213) 439-9690 ext. 3 **Victoria B. Rogers, Pres.**	Programs in San Gabriel Valley that reach greatest # of people with promise of making a measurable impact	$550 to $5 million	Letter of inquiry mailed	Funding decisions are board driven & change as board changes	Need to research current board
Preliminary app. between May 1 and August 15. Response in two days Full app. by invitation due by midnight CDT Aug. 15	**Union Pacific Foundation** www.up.com/found. grants.html 1400 Douglas Street, Stop 1560 Omaha NE 68179 (402) 544-5600	"Communities located on their railroad lines" Community & civic projects, fine arts "build capacity, increase impact, and operate more efficiently & effectively"	Average grant size less than $10,000 1 year funding	Online for both preliminary and full application	Very little competition in Inland Empire Over $1.1 million for CA in 2009	$8,000 received for Science Fair outreach Apply in 2012

Choosing One Funding Source

To stay true to my belief in writing only one proposal at a time, it's now appropriate to make a decision about which single item in your grants calendar you want to build into an actual proposal. Although one asking for a letter of intent seems like an easy choice, I suggest picking a foundation asking for a full proposal with a relatively close deadline or a simple application form as a starter. In my experience, LOIs are more difficult to write than full proposals since they ask for the same information and require you to condense it into paragraphs instead of pages. That may simply be my opinion however, so choose the most appealing grant maker, and let's begin writing the narrative.

ACTIVITIES

1. Answer two or more who, what, when, where, and how questions for 10 or more potential funding opportunities.
2. Highlight application requirements and key words in a government RFP.
3. Fill in a funding fact sheet for five or more grant makers that meet your initial criteria as potential funding resources.
4. Write assumptions you have made from reading between the lines for at least three funding guidelines.
5. Obtain a list of previous grants made by three or more funders.
6. Obtain samples of successful proposals from at least one grant maker and compare them to samples found randomly online.
7. Develop a grants calendar for the funding sources you have chosen.
8. Prioritize the funders by application deadline or other criteria such as project match or feasibility.
9. Choose one funding source for further work.

12

Writing the Narrative

Three rules of work: Out of clutter find simplicity; from discord find harmony; in the middle of the difficulty lies opportunity.

Albert Einstein

Finally! After designing the project(s) you want funded and finding suitable foundations or government departments that might be interested in such a project, after collecting agreements with partners and determining a budget, you're almost ready to actually write a grant proposal. Take a deep breath and congratulate yourself on getting this far. To remind you of what I said in the first chapter, the writing is the easiest part of preparing a proposal. The end is in sight.

Before You Start Writing

There are, however, a few considerations before you start to write.

- **Choose your highest-priority project.** Proposal writing is not an activity you can multitask. You need to focus your entire energy on one project because a grant proposal is a story in disguise. It has a beginning, a middle, and an end. It's filled with drama, tension, and a cast of characters. There are challenges to solve and solutions that sometimes lead to more dilemmas. Most of all, there is a passionate belief that begs to be told and understood. Telling this story requires your full concentration.

A grant proposal is also a technical document, however, filled with arcane facts assembled to elicit an investment of money in what you think is a worthy cause. It uses statistical charts and graphs to document a pressing need. It cites research-based methods to offer answers to a previously unsolved problem. It promises a cost-effective solution to a perplexing scientific or social problem. Again, this needs concentration to select and organize exactly the right information to bring a single story to life.

The secret to proposal writing, if there is one, is to find the balance between passion and logic to present a compelling argument in favor of funding your project—all within a concise, tightly structured framework provided by an outside source. Don't worry; writing a grant proposal is not difficult if you focus on one request at a time.

- **Choose your highest-priority funding source.** Writing one letter and submitting it to a dozen different foundations will result in a dozen rapid responses—all of them saying no. To increase your success in winning grants, you need to pay personal attention to every funder as the individuals they are. You've done your research to know what makes each one unique, and now is the time to use that information. Picture the person or group of people who will be reading your proposal and write directly to them.

- **Carefully reread the guidelines or RFP.** Highlight section headings and key words if you haven't already done so. Print a copy of the application form if there is one, but *do not fill in the blanks of an online proposal yet*. This will be your outline whether you're writing a letter of inquiry or a full proposal. You will use the section headings in the exact order they are printed whether they make sense or not. You will repeat key phrases even if they make you nauseous. You will determine the number of pages per section depending on the number of points each section receives in the scoring. This is not the time to be creative. You will probably do several drafts in a Word document and when it's nearly perfect, you will transfer the words online or create a hard copy of a letter of inquiry that meets both the spirit and the requirements of the funding source.

- **Create a backward calendar.** Start with the funder's deadline and type *your* deadline for a week or 10 days earlier. Unexpected crises always materialize, and some sections will take longer to write than you anticipated so give yourself plenty of time to deal with them. Use the RFP and your knowledge of the material you have already collected to estimate how long each section will take. Again, allow yourself more time than you

Date	Task	Source of Material
Timeline for Writing Narrative		
	Format document	Guidelines
	Write mission, history, and board description	Files & brochures, E.D.'s draft
	Describe current programming	Program director's draft
	Write needs section	My files and drafts
	Write goals and objectives	Draft approved by E. D.
	Write proposed program description	Files, Prog. Dir.'s draft
	Write evaluation process	Exec. & Prog. Dir.'s drafts
	Write staffing and administration paragraph	Personnel
	Write anticipated impact and importance	My files and drafts
	Adapt organization chart	Office Manager's files
	List partners and their contributions	Files
	Create program logic model	Me
	Finalize project budget	Accounting, my files
	Write budget narrative	My notes
	Write sustainability plan, list other funders	My files, E.D.
	Write executive summary	Me
	Complete cover sheet	Me
	Get copies of 501(c)(3) letter, audit, board list, etc.	My files
	Prepare required attachments	My drafts
	Get feedback from trusted readers	Exec. & prog. directors, Susan
	Revise	Me
	Review against guidelines, revise if needed	Me
	Review against scoring criteria, revise	Me
	Produce finished copy	Office manager
	Proofread, make corrections	Someone who hasn't seen it yet
	INTERNAL DEADLINE	
	Final reading against guidelines & checklist	Me and office manager
	Assemble attachments	Me and office manager
	Final assembly of all elements	Team effort
	SUBMIT ELECTRONICALLY OR IN PAPER FORM	
	FUNDER'S DEADLINE	

think you'll need. A calendar for writing a letter of inquiry to a foundation might look like that shown in the timeline chart.

The list may be longer for a full proposal and will certainly be longer for a government grant, but the elements will be essentially the same. You'll notice I'm assuming you've asked other people to write first drafts of some sections and help out with specific tasks. This is where you may need some of that extra time because it's sometimes difficult to merge contributions from several people, I've found, however, that the benefits of having extra hands and brains far outweigh the small hassles. You'll also notice I've listed the submittal date before the funder's deadline. I'll talk more about that in the next chapter but be sure to add that to your planning.

- **Fill in the dates.** Start with the funder's deadline; determine your personal deadline; list the current date; then jiggle and juggle dates to fill in the rest of the chart. Because you have other responsibilities, some items will be grouped together and there will be considerable time gaps between others. Consult a calendar for weekends and holidays, but expect to work during some of them, especially if time is tight.

- **Collect all the relevant documents.** This includes first drafts of sections you and other people have written, notes to yourself, brainstorming summaries, attachments, information about partners, audit, files that you have been filling—everything you might need as a reference once you start writing. Scan them briefly and make a few notes so you can find items easily when you want to, but don't spend a lot of time rereading this information. You simply want to have everything in one place even if that place used to be an empty spot on the floor or a temporary table.

- **Create a format for the narrative section of the proposal.** You can purchase narrative formats from several consultants on the Internet, but I find it's easy to do one myself and I want the security of knowing the outline fits the current version of the guidelines or RFP. Follow the funder's guidelines to the letter. Deal with technical issues like margins, headers and footers, line spacing, font size, etc., first because you can be disqualified for ignoring them and you don't want to reformat everything at the last minute. If the directions say to use 1-inch margins, set your margins for 1-inch, not 0.9-inch. If the RFP says double space using 12-point Times Roman font, do just that. This is not the time or place to be creative.

The most important aspects of the formatting are the section headings and subheadings. Again use the exact words the funder uses in the same order used in the RFP even if you think the narrative would flow better if

Section C came before Section A. Include a subheading for everything they mention in each section and follow their lead for when to use capital letters, bold face, italics, underlining, etc. When you have all the words in order, look at the page count and rating sheet to determine the weight given to each section of the narrative. In a foundation application, you can usually tell this by the amount of white space left after each question or the number of pages specified in the request for an LOI. A federal RFP will be very direct and spell out exactly how many points each section and subsection can receive. Set up your format to mirror this matrix exactly. Type the possible score in huge, 72-point numbers at the beginning of each section. You will delete it later, of course, but this needs to be figural while you're writing. You don't want to waste three pages on a section that has a maximum of 5 points and then squeeze information into a single page when another section carries a possibility of 20 points. I sometimes put these notes to myself in a bright color at the top of each page so they are constantly in front of me and I remember to remove them later. This sometimes takes up a precious line but it forces me to be concise, and it's okay to use less space then allowed but *never* permissible to use more.

If this scenario pushes the anxiety buttons and throws you into panic mode, think of writing a proposal as following a new recipe. Adding a tablespoon of curry to the chicken salad completely changes the taste intended by the directions for a teaspoon. Substituting cinnamon can have a similar effect. Remember the lumps when you added flour directly to the hot gravy before dissolving it in a little cold water? Recipe directions and narrative instructions are written with a purpose in mind, even it they don't make sense to you. Follow them down to the smallest detail, and you'll find guests will rave about your macadamia chip cookies and reviewers will fund your request for a sizeable grant.

Now You're Ready to Write

Find a quiet time and place and start putting all of the pieces together on paper. Turn off your cell phone and block your inbox. Hang a *Do Not Disturb* sign on your door or disappear to an unannounced location for a day or two. Open the narrative file you just created on your computer and start writing. Don't consult your notes or other files. Write from the passion that started this process. Write as if you're talking to someone in person. Don't worry about the statistics or exact titles. Don't worry about spelling, grammar, punctuation, or any of the other "rules" we learned in grade school. This first draft of the narrative wants to capture the simplicity, harmony, and opportunity Einstein is talking about—and you're the only one who can do it. Listen to Maya Angelou when she says, "The idea is to write it so that people hear it and it slides through the brain and goes straight to the heart."

Other hints for keeping the keys clicking and the internal editor at bay as you write your first draft are:

- **Use internal abbreviations.** While you will not use acronyms in the finished document, use them liberally while you're writing the first draft. Make up your own shorthand for words and phrases that you know you will use often. At the end of the day (when you're checking Spell Check's messages), simply use the "find and replace" editing function of your word processing program, and the corrections are made.

- **Leave holes.** When you know you have the information but can't find it easily, or don't want to interrupt the flow of writing, insert a long dash (_____), your initials (MAP) or another signal to return later to fill in the blanks. Again, a simple search command will identify your notes to yourself so you can add the needed material.

- **Don't count words or pages.** Yes, you will be held to a rigid page length when you submit your proposal, but don't worry about it until later in the process. It's more important to make sure you include everything you want to say than to edit at the beginning. I've also found it's much easier to cut pages than to add them, even when vigorous pruning is necessary. Having said that, if you're accustomed to writing a 25-page proposal for a federal grant and the guidelines change to limit the pages to 12, don't try to cut and paste an earlier proposal. It's easier, and the narrative will flow more smoothly if you start from scratch.

Writing Is Revising

One key to writing a proposal that achieves Maya Angelou's goal is to recognize that you will be reading and revising this document several times. Each time you revisit it—and each time you ask someone else to read it—you will change a few things. Expect to do this, and you'll have the tight, carefully constructed letter of inquiry or proposal narrative you want to submit. If you expect to produce a finished product in one marathon sitting, you'll be sorely disappointed in the results. Refer back to the narrative timeline on page 179 and you'll see how many times I added "edit and revise" to the list. You may have more or fewer revisions than I do, but don't leave editing out of the equation.

When you finish the first draft, put the narrative away for a few days, then print a hard copy and read it as if you know nothing about the field you've written about. Author and writing coach Sheila Bender (www.writingitreal.com) has developed a three-step critique method for personal essays and poetry that I've adapted slightly to use for editing grant proposals.

- **Highlight the Velcro words and phrases.** These are the words that jump off the page and stick to you. These are also the words the reviewers will remember. Look for phrases you want them to jot on their scoring sheets.

- **Track the flow of your feelings.** Do you feel the tensions in the community as outlined in the needs section or are you bored by numbers? Are you excited when you read about the proposed project? Do you sense the stability of the agency or do you pick up undertones of trouble? Read slowly and jot your emotions in the margins as you experience them and as they change.

- **Identify points of confusion where you want more information.** Look for jargon, long sentences, words of more than three syllables, and ideas that wandered into unnecessary territory. Check for things you left out that need to be included. Highlight them with a different color than the Velcro words or make margin notes with a different pen.

When you return to your computer to revise your first draft, use the information you gained in this first critique. Emphasize the Velcro words you want to keep and soften those you want to diminish. Remove duplicate words. Rewrite awkward sentences. If a typed sentence runs more than three lines, chop it in two. Use 10-cent words rather than dollar ones. Replace all forms of the verb "to be" with action words.

Seeking Outside Feedback

This is a good time to ask people who contributed first drafts to read the proposal. Encourage them to read the whole document using Sheila Bender's three-step process and then return to the section they know the best to check for factual accuracy. It's also a good idea to ask someone who is in a totally different field to read it and give you their impressions, particularly noting places they don't understand. Even if you're asking for money for an esoteric branch of nuclear biology, a layperson must be able to make sense of your request because someone with only a smidgen of knowledge of your specialty may sit on your review panel. A banker, business executive, or lawyer is a good reader for social services proposals. They will not be bashful in telling you if your plan is vague or too "touchy-feely."

- **Edit and revise again**. Use the feedback you received, but don't let outsiders change the direction of your proposal. You're looking for clarity, not program design. If the evaluator insists on using technical terms you don't understand, work together long enough to reach a happy medium. If the banker says the facility rental needs to be doubled, do a bit more research about market values. If the program director, however, wants to substitute guest artists for a drumming circle, file that information for your next proposal.

- **Proofread!** Keep Spell Check working at all times, but correct mistakes at the end of each day so you don't interrupt the flow of your writing. Before you share what you've written with someone else, read it aloud to yourself. Often the to/too/two and other common mistakes Spell Check doesn't catch will jump off the page. As a final step, however, this is a job best delegated to another person. You will have read the words so many times, you have almost memorized them and you will read what you meant to say rather than what is on the page. If you have time, it doesn't hurt to have several pairs of eyes proofread the final copy.

Basic Writing Skills Are Important

Although your focus needs to be on content, attention to standard rules of spelling, punctuation, and sentence construction must also be followed. If you're weak in one of these areas, review your copy of Strunk and White's *Elements of Style* or seek help from someone who reads *The Chicago Manual of Style* for pleasure. Key principles for writing a grant proposal include the following.

- **Avoid jargon and acronyms unless they are used by the funding agency—** and then use them sparingly. Write as if your reader is only vaguely familiar with your area of interest. If you must use jargon, explain what it means in plain English the first time you use it. The same rule applies to acronyms, especially if you use them to shorten the name of your agency or project.

- **Vary the structure of your sentences.** Keep both sentences and paragraphs short. Let me repeat the advice to cut sentences that run over three lines in half. Similarly, if you discover a paragraph that contains more than eight typewritten lines, consider dividing it into smaller segments. A corollary is to use active voice, which is more concise than the passive, and a positive statement, which is more effective than a negative one.

- **Use graphics.** Bullets and numbered lists are the most basic means of consolidating information and adding variety to the page so use them frequently. Add copies of your organization chart and program logic model. Also consider charts, graphs, diagrams, and other visual elements that *show* rather than *tell* the story of the identified needs, program activities, and budget. These devices actually save more space than they take and are often easier to understand.

- **Use a thesaurus sparingly.** Funders like to see the words they've carefully chosen in their mission statements and funding priorities used, so be careful about substituting synonyms. Having said that, do vary the words you know you use frequently and translate convoluted statements into simple English.

- **Watch your language.** Although jokes abound about our obsession with politically correct language, it's important to be sensitive with word choice.

  - Are the people who will make use of your services participants? Members? Clients? Subjects? Young people? Children in grades K to 12? Children aged birth to five? Choose one and use it consistently.

  - Use plural pronouns instead of struggling with he/she variations.

  - Remember people *have* a disability or condition. They are not defined by it. Use "clients with diabetes" rather than "diabetics."

  - Go easy with superlatives. You want to paint a graphic picture of the need for your project, but don't go overboard and describe a scene from Dickens. Because people have limited incomes does not mean they are hopeless, pitiful, forgotten, depressed, immoral, or vegetating. And although your program is worthy of funding, I doubt it is stellar, one-of-a-kind, precedent-shattering, or awe-inspiring. You are writing a request for funding, not an advertisement for a new toothpaste and words like these cast doubt on your credibility as a serious professional.

- **Pay attention to beginnings and endings.** Never start or end a thought on a weak note. Place strong sentences at the beginning and ending of paragraphs and sections. Place strong words at the beginning and ending of sentences. Every time you see a "this," "it," or other vague word, find a better one.

Final Steps

You've heard the expression "The devil is in the details," and that is definitely true for grant proposals. He lurks in most unexpected places, so check and double-check your revisions. Make sure numbers have the correct amount of zeroes. Watch your cutting and pasting to make sure everything moved where you wanted it to. Above all, ask again and again and again if your words answer the questions the funder is asking. When you're finished, remove those colored formatting guidelines you created at the beginning and move to the next step of assembling the entire proposal packet.

ACTIVITIES

1. Choose one project and one funding source. Carefully reread the RFP or guidelines and highlight questions to be answered in the narrative.

2. Create a timeline for writing the narrative section of the proposal allowing for external feedback and several revisions.

3. Gather all material that is relevant to this particular project and funding source in one easily accessible place.

4. Format pages of the narrative to correspond to the RFP guidelines and to reflect the scoring matrix.

5. Write the first draft of the narrative section of the proposal.

6. Edit the first draft using the three-step process of identifying Velcro words, tracking feelings, and noticing places of confusion and/or need for more information. Write the second draft accordingly.

7. Inset at least three tables, charts, graphs, or other graphic portrayals of information.

8. Revise narrative to meet space and formatting parameters.

9. Obtain feedback on current revision from at least three people. Revise to incorporate their feedback.

10. Review RFP guidelines and scoring matrix and revise if necessary.

11. Proofread and remove formatting reminders.

chapter **13**

Submitting Your Proposal

If it weren't for the last minute, a lot of things wouldn't get done.

Michael S. Taylor

The last week before you submit your proposal to the foundation or government agency will seem like purgatory. You've finally squeezed the narrative into 25 pages when someone discovers three paragraphs describing staff training that *must* be included. The president had emergency surgery for gallstones but her husband says he'll take the papers she needs to sign to the hospital if he remembers. One of your partners has gotten cold feet and isn't really sure they want to provide a psychologist for the project. A power surge wiped out your executive summary, and a volunteer spilled coffee on the collection of assurances that were already dated and signed.

Maybe all of these things won't happen at once, but be prepared for at least one calamity to strike just when you think you're ready to mail the packet or press the "send" button. Unfortunately, there is little to prevent these unexpected glitches from happening except to allow yourself plenty of time to deal with them. You *will* meet your deadline, even though you may have to jump through some hurdles you didn't see coming.

Taking Care of Yourself

Now is the time to arrange things so you and the proposal are as close to the center of the universe as possible. Don't schedule any meetings and postpone those that are already scheduled. Put other projects on hold until after the proposal is mailed. Lay in a store of comfort food that is easy to prepare. Exercise every day or at least get up and walk around a bit. Get plenty of sleep. In short, do all the things you know you should do to take care of yourself so you don't end up sabotaging your efforts by getting sick. In the grant world, deadlines are deadlines. There are no excuses allowed for a proposal that arrives at 12:01 PST when the instructions said 12:00 EST, and you have dozens of last-minute details that need your attention before that time arrives.

Moving Past the Narrative

While the narrative is the major writing segment of the proposal, you also need to prepare the other documents on the checklist that usually is included in the RFP instructions. (If there isn't one, create one so you don't overlook a vital ingredient.) Here's where I usually multitask and assemble things as I can fit them into my other responsibilities

- **Budget and Budget Narrative:** Although some standardization of budget forms is beginning to take place and many Excel spreadsheets are included in application packets, there still seem to be as many differences as there are similarities. If you understand numbers and accounting, the forms will make sense to you, and you will have little trouble transferring information from your worksheets to the prescribed format. If you don't understand numbers and accounting, get someone who does to fill in the blanks. In both cases, your major concern is the budget narrative, which translates those numbers into tangible objects and services.

  Narrative is rather a misleading term since the funder is not asking for long paragraphs of information. Simple phrases are adequate. If there is a single figure in the personnel column, break it out into positions with the percent of time spent on the project noted. If the mileage amount looks high, note the radius of your service area and the fact that a key program element is biweekly home visits to parents with medically fragile infants. If your facility rental is particularly low for the area, explain the arrangement with another agency to use their pool during non-peak hours in exchange for the use of your van. Assume the people who review the finances will not see the rest of the proposal so give them the details they need to see what's beneath the numbers. As often as possible, tie the dollar amounts to program objectives so they can easily figure out your program is cost effective.

Finally, don't forget to include a list of other grants you have received, funds that are pending, and other major donors even if the money is not specifically for this project.

- **Executive Summary:** This will be a test of your ability to condense a complex process into a tiny, tiny package. Just as Twitter restricts your Tweet to 140 characters, most funders restrict your executive summary to 250 words. Into this tiny capsule, you need to give *all* the reasons for them to fund your project—and it can't be a simple list. Start with your highly refined purpose statement and refer to your program logic model to add phrases about each of the other key elements in your proposal. To remind you of what they are, here is a quick checklist:
  - The need or problem you have identified
  - How your goals and objectives will address this problem
  - Target audience
  - Community and agency resources
  - Implementation activities and timeline
  - Importance and impact of projected outcomes
  - Agency's history and demonstration of ability to implement proposal
  - Staffing
  - Collaborative partnerships
  - Performance measurements and evaluation
  - Total funds requested shown to be cost effective
  - Future funding strategies.

  When you realize I used 71 words to construct this list, you begin to realize the challenge of writing the executive summary. Focus on your purpose statement and logic model and you'll be able to do it, although it may take several attempts and much revision.

- **Cover Sheet:** Although you may be tempted to fill in the blanks in this innocuous-looking form at the beginning of the process, don't. Wait until the end so you are sure the dollar amount you are requesting is firm, the project funds from other sources are realistic, and you can further condense your 250-word executive summary into 50 words. This program description will be used by the funder in their reports, in public relations activities, and possibly on their web page, so consider it a simple expansion of your core purpose statement and make the words sing of passion and commitment to solving a persistent problem we all can identify.

- **Cover Letter:** If you are submitting a proposal by mail to a foundation, you will need to enclose a cover letter that is different from both the cover sheet and the executive summary. The primary purpose of this one-page letter typed on your letterhead is to tie the agency's mission and the project's purpose to the funder's interests. If you have received a grant from this foundation or are currently receiving funds from them, thank them for their support and give a short description of the impact and importance of their assistance. If they are a new funder, give just enough background to set the scene and establish your credibility before you explain your current project. In both situations, focus on a few key activities and the reasons you are asking for funding. In this case, save your core program summary to use as a strong ending to sum up the purpose of the proposed project.

- **Attachments and Assurances:** The RFP will contain a list of the attachments they want and copies or links to the assurances. The important thing is to assemble and number them in the order they are listed. It sounds like a small matter, but this is no time to be rebellious. Follow the rules here and use Roman numerals, capital letters, lowercase letters, etc. Use whatever is called for in each section—and then double-check your work. Someone on the receiving end will have a checklist and they will notice.

Submitting the Documents

Once again, the details for how the funder wants to receive the proposal package will be spelled out in the RFP or guidelines. There are only a few things to be wary of in this step of the process.

- **Confirm the address.** It's usually very easy to tell if the proposal is to be sent electronically or by mail but double-check the address because some funders have different addresses for different purposes. This is particularly true for federal grants where the RFP is available on Grants.gov, but the proposal is to be submitted to a particular agency or department.

- **Don't wait until the last minute.** Some funders allow postmarked time stamps and make allowances for Internet queues but don't count on it. *All* funders are rigorous in adhering to deadlines, and you don't want your hard work to go to waste because you were two minutes late. Plan on submitting your proposal a week to ten days before it's due and you'll be okay.

- **Use paper clips instead of staples to hold pages together, and don't worry about fancy covers and bindings if you submit hard copies.** Proposals are often taken apart with sections given to different groups of people to review.

- **Review everything one last time before you seal the packet or push the "send" key.** You are checking to make sure everything is included and in the right order in a mailed packet and you are checking to make sure every blank is filled in an online application. You know if a computer sees a blank space, they reject the file so write something in each box even if it is an explanation of how this doesn't apply to you or is information repeated from the line above. Also look at the visual appearance of the material to make sure you didn't triple space when you meant to double space and that the submitted copy looks like the version on your computer screen.

Preparing for an On-site Visit

Some foundations, particularly local family and community foundations, would like to visit your site to see programs in action before they make their final decision. This is a wonderful opportunity to build an ongoing relationship and demonstrate the effectiveness of your work, but you need to plan carefully for it. Let me close this chapter with a story to describe what can go wrong.

My oldest grandson serves on the youth panel of a foundation that sets aside $60,000 each year for teens to allocate to local charities. The application and selection process is the same for both the adult and youth panels. Each year, funding priorities are reviewed and revised if necessary; guidelines are changed accordingly, and an RFP is widely distributed. Small review teams rank the applicants, conduct agency visits, and present both written and oral recommendations to the full teen panel who act as a whole to make the final decisions.

Last year, he was looking forward to an on-site visit to an organization that helps recent immigrants learn English and U.S. ways of life while respecting their rich cultural heritage. He had heard they demonstrated their work by serving food from their country of origin, sharing ethnic dance and folk stories, and teaching the visitors a few words of their native language. The director of the agency was sick but their scheduled visit was held as planned. The food was delicious but the children who served it didn't know the ingredients or what spice produced the distinctive flavor. The dances were colorful and performed with grace and charm, but the dancers could not explain their meaning or cultural significance of their movements or identify the instruments in the recorded music. The president of the board greeted them warmly—and left early for another engagement. The remaining staff could not answer questions about other programs, financial accountability, or short- or long-term agency goals. In spite of a three-year history of funding, a well-written program that spoke to the funder's priorities, and a pleasant evening, the agency did not receive funds last year.

I know teens can hold adults to extremely high standards, and they may have been harsh in this case, but I think my grandson's blunt comments reflect what many reviewers consider but seldom say out loud.

- *An agency has to be more than one person. If the director had had a heart attack instead of the flu, who would continue the programs?*

- *We were looking for change and understanding, not a bunch of painted performers doing cute tricks.*

- *When we go to a restaurant, my dad asks the servers how the food is prepared and if the fish is fresh or frozen. If one of the objectives of the program is to teach young people born in this country to maintain traditions from another country, we expected them to at least know the main ingredients of the meal they served us. They didn't even know if we were eating chicken or pork or that each family has its own curry recipe.*

- *When the president left, we were all shocked. If our visit was not a priority for him, why should his agency be a priority for us? We had requests for $234,000 and only $60,000 to grant. His leaving made our decision much easier.*

- *I was really disappointed we couldn't give them any money because I think kids my age need to know their cultural heritage and I think they probably do a pretty good job of that just by getting kids together in the same room to compare notes about their parents' lives as compared to theirs. That's my guess, though, and I'm not willing to give away money on my guess. They needed to show us to convince us—and they didn't do that.*

I think that about sums up the essence of grant writing. Basically, people and organizations who give away grants are no different from people and organizations who accept grants. They both want to move forward in realizing a strong passion. They want to see the funds being used effectively and efficiently. They want to see results. And like grant recipients, funders often look for evidence of success in informal, reading-between-the-lines ways. Make sure your proposal embodies these common sense truths.

Celebrating

But let's not end on a down note. You're exhausted, and so is everyone around you. Maybe you just want to crawl into a cave and not talk to anyone for a month. Not so fast! You need to do something out of the ordinary to mark the successful completion of a major accomplishment. You have to admit pushing that "send" key and then watching the computer screen go blank is terribly anticlimactic, so grab a couple of people, whoop and holler, go out for Thai food or juicy steaks, and celebrate the occasion. You can get back to work tomorrow.

ACTIVITIES

1. List six ways you'll take care of yourself in the final days of preparing a grant proposal.

2. Transfer financial information from your worksheets to a form provided by a funder.

3. Write a budget narrative to explain major expenditures.

4. List other grants and major donations you have received or are applying for.

5. Write an executive summary in 250 words or less.

6. Write a cover letter to accompany your proposal to the foundation you have chosen.

7. Locate or prepare a checklist of items to be included in the submittal package.

8. Sketch elements you would include in an on-site visit from a funder.

9. Plan a way to celebrate the moment the proposal is in the mail or sent via email.

chapter **14**

Following Up and Starting Over

One must know not just how to accept a gift, but with what grace to share it.

Maya Angelou

The most difficult week for me personally in the grant writing process is the first week *after* the proposal has been submitted. The adrenaline rush has evaporated. The stacks of paper and loose ends remain to clutter up my office. My inbox is full and pink phone messages seem to be a mile high. I know there's nothing more to do for this project except wait for a response—and I'm not particularly good at waiting. Still, there are things that need attention so I take a deep breath and begin again.

Saying Thank You

The first order of business is sending quick email notes, thank-you cards, and phone calls to let everyone who helped in any way know the proposal is successfully on its way. You can never say thank you enough, so be generous—and be sincere. Don't say the same thing to someone who participated in one brainstorming group as you do to the accountant who spent hours helping you figure out how you could pay for both home visitors and a nurse practitioner.

Send copies of the completed proposal with all the attachments to your partners and the person who will be coordinating the project implementation, and prepare a summary for the board members. Promise to let everyone know the outcome when you hear.

Cleaning Up and Filing

You may have established a rudimentary filing system while you were working on the proposal, but now you need to decide what you really want to keep so you can find it again. According to Henry Flood, the director of Research and Development for Drew Management Group, in an article for The Grantsmanship Center, "No single method of organizing grants paperwork and computer files is perfect. The key is to devise a system that makes sense for you . . . [and] to take an approach that will make sense to anyone who might succeed you." Flood suggests a color-coded system of file folders/pockets/envelopes that separates the various functions that make up the grants process. His comprehensive system can be found by typing "grants filing system" in the search engine on The Grantsmanship Center web page (www.tgic.com).

For some people, large three-ring notebooks work better. I use a combination, including lightweight stationery boxes I buy from a printer.

The number and complexity of these files will vary depending on the size of your agency and the scope of your project but I find useful categories are:

- **Organization Background:** I suggest individual files be kept for:
  - The 501(c)(3) tax exemption letter
  - Summary profile of your organization
  - Master list of awarded grants for last five years
  - Copy of most recent audit and organization-wide budget
  - Roster of board members with professional notations
  - Résumés and professional summaries of key staff members.
- **Research:** You will probably want to separate demographics and community needs from program design ideas but other categories may fit your

projects better. Label your divisions to help you file and retrieve information easily.

- **Prospects:** Start with broad groupings like government, foundations, corporations and individuals and then create separate folders or sections for specific funding sources as you find them.

- **Applications:** You may need a banker's box or other sizeable container for the proposals you are currently working on. I subdivide each funding request into the major sections of the proposal, i.e., guidelines/RFP, goals and objectives, need, program design, staffing, budget, community resources, staffing, partnerships, budget, evaluation, sustainability, assurances.

- **Grant Administration:** After the proposal is submitted, return documents to other categories for future use and file a complete submittal package alphabetically by funding source. If an award is granted, move the material to an active location and add:

  - Correspondence

  - Award letter and grant agreement

  - Copy of approved budget and narrative

  - Finance and performance reports with any audit information

- **Resources:** While this is not exactly the "junk drawer," it looks amazingly like my bottom drawer since it contains articles on fundraising in general, information on books and other publications that look interesting, subscription records, conference and workshop notes, etc. I'm always surprised at how often I search this collection to find the name of the speaker I heard several years ago who was working on an evaluation tool that sounded promising or find the research data that fits this proposal perfectly. Some things never go out of date.

Pamela Grow, the creator of Simple Development Systems, one of the first online programs geared to the busy fundraiser in the one-person development shop, invites readers of her blog (www.pamelasgrantwritingblog.com/) to paste the following form on the inside cover of the file folder that holds the original copy of each proposal she submits. This provides an instant overview of the status of each application.

Funding Source, Project		
Foundation Funder:	Website	Phone
Funding Contact/Title:		
General Operating or Project–Name:		New Renewal
Identify Board connection (if any):		
Timeline		
Deadline	Date Application Mailed	
	Anticipated Funding Decision	
IF Declined		
Submission entered in database?	Declination Date:	
Thank–you letter sent:		
Follow–up phone call (if declined):		
Questions to funder:		
1. Is there anything we could have done differently in our proposal?		
2. May we resubmit for your next funding cycle?		
3. Are you aware of any other foundations that we might approach?		
Resubmission Date:		
Financial		
Amount Requested:	Amount Awarded:	
Date of Award Letter:		
Report Due:		
Thank–you letter sent:		
Notes:		

Waiting Patiently

Don't bother calling or pacing the floor waiting for a response from the funder. They have a process to complete that takes time and they will get back to you according to their own schedule. Use this time to set things in motion for implementing the project when you do get the funds or applying for other grants if your proposal is rejected. If you will be the one coordinating the project, you'll begin the start-up activities you outlined in the proposal like meeting with partners, creating supply lists, refining program ideas, establishing accounting systems, setting up evaluation protocols, etc. If you are handing over implementation to other staff, make sure they have complete copies of the proposal and relevant background materials and then back away graciously to return to your other responsibilities.

Responding to Yes or No

If the answer is yes, write a note to the funder thanking them for the grant and giving a preview of how the project will be implemented, then turn the rest over to the person coordinating the activities. If it's a government grant, that person will also be responsible for negotiating the terms of the contract so you can turn to your next task, which is notifying the people you said you'd get back to when you heard the results. Thank them for their support, introduce the project coordinator and give a preview of the timeline for the next few months.

If the answer is no, feel and express your disappointment for a few days, then write the thank-you letters. Try not to take the rejection personally. There are a dozen reasons, but if you produced a quality proposal and met the deadline, the most likely reason is that they had more requests than they had money so they had to make some difficult decisions. You will want to learn why your proposal was denied, however, so you can make some adjustments next time. Under the Freedom of Information Act, government funders must give you the reasons for a grant decision, but you may have to request it in writing and you may have to wait a while for it. Foundations are under no such obligation but many are willing to share so if you applied to a foundation, call your contact person to thank them for their consideration and ask for feedback on why your proposal was denied. Call out of sense of curiosity rather than anger or disappointment to learn what you can do to modify the project to more closely match their interests and/or to explore other programs they might consider—and be sure to take notes to use when preparing the next proposal.

And you will go on to the next proposal. You have other options in your funding chart to explore and you've been collecting more possibilities as you continue your resource collecting as an ongoing activity.

Staying Current

Now that you know the process, it's important that you continue to research funding sources, develop potential program designs, and apply for more grants. As you've no doubt discovered, an important element of this is making and maintaining contacts in both your professional field and the fundraising arena.

Dr. Ivan Misner, the founder and CEO of Business Network International (BNI), encourages sole proprietors and small business owners to become an active member in six distinct communities:

1. Trade or professional association
2. Chamber of Commerce
3. Service club
4. Business Networking Group whose focus is giving and getting appropriate referrals
5. An online social networking site
6. Church, woodworking/quilting/photography or other personal or leisure-time group

Joining six groups may seem like a huge expenditure of money and time for a small return until you consider the worth of the number of contacts you make and the resources you will discover.

To adapt this concept to searching for grants, consider exploring the following activities:

- Subscribe to funding alerts, e-zines, and blogs that focus on philanthropy, grants, fundraising, etc., like those listed in the resource section, and make it a habit to browse them at a regular time each week.
- Visit a meeting of your local chapter of the Grants Professional Assoication (formerly American Association of Grant Professionals at www .grantprofessionals.org) or the Association of Fundraising Professionals (AFP at www.afpnet.org) and consider joining them.
- Update your agency's web site and explore online social networking sites.
- Become familiar with the business community by joining the Chamber of Commerce.
- Visit agencies doing similar work when you travel.

Enjoy! There are some wonderful people who seek grant funds for causes they feel passionate about—and there are an equal number of wonderful people who have money to support those causes. Now that you have a taste of how to access that world, make the most of it and meet more and more of these wonderful people. I sincerely hope I can meet *you* someday by email, letter, comment on my blog, or even in person. Until then, may all your wishes be granted.

Glossary

2-1-1 Three-digit phone number to call for health and social service information and referrals almost every place in the United States.

501(c)(3) Section of the IRS code that designates an organization as charitable and tax exempt. The vast majority of foundations require grant recipients to be 501(c)(3) organizations.

Accountability The responsibility of the organization to keep a donor informed about the use that is made of the donor's gift as well as the cost of raising it.

Affinity Group An independent coalition of grantmaking, community service, or research organizations or individuals that share information and provide professional development and networking opportunities. Members of such groups may be collaborators or competitors when seeking funds.

Allowable Costs Project costs that are necessary for project implementation.

American FactFinder Source of detailed statistics the Census Bureau collects in the official census held every ten years and the many population and economic surveys conducted in the interim.

Annual Report Voluntary publication produced by foundations and nonprofit organizations to describe their activities and financial position for the past year. Although they range from single typed sheets to elaborate multicolored documents, they are important sources of information about the mission, board membership, funding priorities and amounts, and the financial health of both foundations and other nonprofits.

AOR   Authorized Organizational Representative. One or more staff members identified with the federal government as having authority to submit applications on behalf of an organization.

Articles of Incorporation   Legal document filed with the secretary of state as the first step in forming a nonprofit 501(c)(3) corporation.

"Ask"   The actual request for a specific amount of money in the cover letter or proposal.

Assets   Cash, stock, bond, real estate, and other holdings. Foundations usually invest their assets and use the earned income to make grants.

Assurance of Compliance   Certifications grant seekers must sign and file before they qualify for funding from government agencies covering everything from data management and ownership to treatment of animal and human subjects.

Audit: Financial   Formal examination of an organization's accounting records that is often required by funders.

Audit: Program   Review, often performed by the grant maker, of the outcomes of the grant-funded project with attention paid to compliance with applicable terms, laws, regulations, etc.

Award   Another name for a grant or money given for a specific purpose that does not need to be repaid.

AVO   All Volunteer Organization. If an organization has a 501(c)(3) tax exemption, it can receive foundation and public funds even if it doesn't have a paid staff.

Benefactor   Someone who makes a major financial contribution to an individual artist or nonprofit organization.

Bequest   Money or property directed by a will to a specified person or organization. Many individuals make bequests to community foundations to be used as designated funds for specific purposes. It never hurts to ask if you or your agency qualify for any of this money.

Block Grants   Federal funds given to states, counties, or local municipalities for a particular purpose such as child health services, transportation, or community redevelopment. A common one is the **CDBG (Community Development Block Grant)**, which mandates a percentage of the local money for streets, sewers, parks, lighting, etc., must go to human services. The dollar amounts are generally small but the process is relatively easy, the decision makers know the needs of your community, and the competition is relatively small. A CBDG is often a good place to start for a small agency and/or a novice grant writer.

Board of Directors (Trustees) The elected governing bodies of both foundations and nonprofit corporations that have policy-making, fiduciary, and oversight responsibilities. Proposals need to be approved by both boards before grants can be awarded.

"Bricks-and-Mortar" Slang for a grant for a building or construction grant.

Bridge Loan/Grant Funds to fill a gap in funding, sometimes between the awarding of the grant and the first check, sometimes to pay for services that will later be reimbursed, sometimes as an interim measure for a challenge grant. Bridge loans are secured from a bank or individuals and need to be repaid, usually with interest. Bridge grants are rare but are sometimes available from a funding source with which you have an ongoing relationship.

Bylaws Rules governing the operation of a nonprofit organization.

Capacity Building Grant Funds used to strengthen the infrastructure of an agency so it can better meet its mission. These grants are often awarded for two or more years for activities like board and staff training, computer hardware and software, fund development efforts, salary assessment and modifications, or financial audits.

Capital Campaign An extensive campaign to raise a large amount of money for construction or renovation of a building, purchase of land, or major piece of equipment.

Cash Flow Statement A report of cash receipts and payments during a specified time period, often monthly or quarterly. Financial statements always include a cash flow statement.

Catalytic Philanthropy New form of philanthropy defined by Mark R. Kramer, cofounder and managing director of FSG Social Impact Advisors, where funders take responsibility for achieving results, mobilize a campaign for change, use all available tools including investment capital, advocacy, litigation, and lobbying to create knowledge that leads to action that knits together the pieces of solutions to long-standing issues—an extension of strategic or transformative philanthropy and social entrepreneurship.

CBO Community Based Organization with no religious affiliation that provides human services within a particular community or population.

CCR Central Contractor Registration is required of everyone who does business with the federal government and is a necessary first step in applying for federal funds. A link (www.ccr.gov) and instructions are available at www.Grants.gov.

CFDA Number   Catalog of Federal Domestic Assistance number, which identifies a specific federal grant program. The CFDA is the encyclopedia of funding programs.

CFRB   Code of Federal Regulations. All of the rules and requirements published by administrative agencies and department like DOD (Department of Defense), NIH (National Institutes of Health), DOE (Department of Energy), etc.

Challenge Grant   A grant made to "challenge" the organization to raise additional funds. If the funds are not raised, the grant is not awarded.

COLA   Cost-of Living Adjustment tied to the Consumer Price Index that is added to salaries to keep pace with inflation.

Collaboration   Partners who have come together from different organizations or disciplines to work on a mutually beneficial project or program. Members can include public and private organizations, government agencies, and individuals.

Community Assessment   Identification of the needs and resources of a particular geographic region or population.

Community Foundation   Public foundation that combines and manages funds from many different donors to make grants in a specific geographic region. Usually the donors' funds remain intact and grants are made from the interest on investments.

Competitive Grants   Grants awarded on merit rather than on financial need.

Concept Map   A diagram showing the relationships among concepts in much the same way that a sentence diagram represents the grammar of a sentence— Uses phrases such as "results in," "contributes to," "is required by," "between," "includes," etc., to show the connections.

Conditional Grant   A funding source agrees to pay part of the total costs of a project on the condition that funds for the remainder of the project are secured from other sources. For example Foundation A may fund donor tracking software if the grant for new computers is granted by Foundation B or raised through a designated appeal. The grant may also be withheld pending receiving permission for required materials or procedures, having a sufficient number of participants, securing appropriate space, or other nonmonetary conditions.

Continuum of Care (CofC)   An array of seamless services from basic support to independent self-sufficiency for projects focusing on homelessness, domestic violence, substance abuse, juvenile justice, etc. The continuum flows in the opposite direction from independent living to total care for many senior, health-care and other projects that focus on the end of life. CofCs can also be smaller in scope and involve seamless transitions between projects and programs within and between agencies.

Corporate Foundation   Private foundation that derives its grant-making funds primarily from the contributions of a profit-making business. The mission of the foundation and the goals of the corporation are usually complimentary but the organizations remain legally separate.

Corporate Giving Program   Grant-making program established and administered *within* a profit-making company. Larger corporations often have both a corporate giving program and a corporate foundation. Corporate foundations often has a broader mission and geographic range. Corporate giving programs tends to focus on local needs surrounding their headquarters and places of operation, has more flexible parameters and is frequently a source for product donations.

Cost-Benefit Analyses   Comparison of the costs and benefits of a project or program to determine whether the benefits merit the cost. Also used to compare programs to see which maximize net benefits.

Cover Letter   Letter accompanying a grant proposal to introduce the organization and summarize the proposal. This is different from a letter of intent, which is a mini-proposal.

Cultivation   Development of an ongoing relationship with a donor, program officer, elected official, or other potential funding source before and after requesting and receiving funds.

Declining/Decreasing Grant   A multiyear grant that becomes smaller each year in expectation that the ongoing funds will be raised from other sources.

Demonstration Grant   Money to establish an innovative program that can serve as a model and be replicated if successful. Meticulous records of procedures and findings are extremely important for this type of grant as is the ability and willingness to share information and train others.

Determination Letter   Official letter from the IRS stating the organization has tax-exempt status. Since there are several categories of exemption, you want your letter to grant 501(c)(3) status.

Designated Funds   Restricted money to be spent according to the specifications of the grantor. All grant funds are considered designated for the agency and require separate accounting and accountability. The proposal becomes the expected performance standards for funds received from a foundation. A government grant will have additional requirements for program implementation, record keeping, and reporting.

Discretionary Funds   Funds distributed at the discretion of the funder. Almost every funding source, including all branches of the government, have discretionary funds that may lie outside their guidelines and often do not entail a complicated decision process. After a solid relationship has been established with a foundation or program officer, it's appropriate to ask if discretionary funds are available and what they can be used for. This may be a source of funds in an emergency or for a quirky project, but it is always a long shot and should never be your first request.

Dissemination   Method by which you will inform others of your project and its outcome.

Distribution Committee   The group responsible for making final grant recommendations or decisions. Sometimes committees are a combination of staff and volunteers who make a recommendation to a board of directors who make the final decision that the committee then implements. Sometimes a foundation board grants all powers to the committee. In government grants, proposals are reviewed by volunteer panels, and the distribution committee ensures eligibility, handles appeals, and makes final decisions.

Donor-Advised Fund   A fund held by a community foundation where the donor, or a committee appointed by the donor, recommends eligible recipients for grants from the fund.

Donor-Designated Fund   A fund held by a community foundation where the donor, or a committee appointed by the donor, specifically determines how funds and/or assets are to be used.

Double Bottom Line   The measurement of both social and financial returns on investments.

Due Diligence   This is a legal term denoting "the degree of prudence that might be properly expected from a reasonable person in the circumstances." While this usually refers to fiduciary matters, due diligence is increasingly applied to other areas of grant management and use.

DUNS   Donor Universal Number System. To submit a grant to the government (and an increasing number of foundations) you will need this nine-digit identification designation received by registering at www.Grants.gov or by calling 1-866-705-5711. Don't confuse this with your EIN number. Both are nine digits and both will be required for the cover page of most applications and many legal documents.

E-Application   An electronic, web-based grant application system now used exclusively for federal grants and by many foundations.

Earned Income   Money not dependent on grants such as fees for service, membership campaigns, product sales, interest on investments, special events, etc. Funders like to see you have a mix of relatively stable income and are not entirely dependent on foundation or government grants.

E-Biz POC   Electronic Business Point of Contact, which is the agency's user account with the federal government. You will also choose a master Personal Identification Number (M-PIM) to identify yourself in all transactions with the government.

EIN   Employer Identification Number assigned by the IRS to all organizations (nonprofit and for profit) with paid employees. Don't confuse this with your DUNS number. Both are nine digits and both will be required for the cover page of most applications and many legal documents.

Employee Matching Grant   A contribution made to a nonprofit organization by an individual that is matched by a contribution from his or her employer.

Empowerment Zone   Small urban and rural geographic areas judged to be in economic distress and therefore eligible for special training, business development, and economic stimulus grants.

Endowment   Money set aside for investments that earn interest to pay for programs and agency operating expenses. Universities, hospitals, museums, and charities with large physical plants are the most common recipients of endowment funds although smaller education and arts agencies, shelters and other social service projects, and some groups that provide scholarships are establishing endowment funds. The government and many foundations exclude endowment requests in their guidelines.

Executive Summary   Section of the proposal that outlines the major reasons for the request, details program objectives and activities, and provides budget overview.

Family Foundations   Independent private foundations whose funds come from members of a single family. Family members often serve as officers and play a major role in grant-making decisions that are frequently very personal. Some have grown very large like the Ford Foundation but most are considerably smaller and make smaller, more local grants. All private foundations, however, must make charitable expenditures of approximately 5 percent of the market value of their assets every year.

FBO   Faith Based Organization that provides human services and is affiliated with a religion or spiritual movement. FBOs cannot use federal funds for religious activities and cannot restrict access to their services based on the religion of the recipient.

Federal Poverty Levels   Income levels below which families are officially considered to be "poor." The levels vary by family size and are adjusted yearly according to changes in the Consumer Price Index.

Federated Giving Program   A joint fundraising effort usually administered by a nonprofit "umbrella" organization that in turn distributes contributed funds to several nonprofit agencies. United Way United Jewish Appeal, the United Negro College Fund, and joint arts councils are examples of federated giving programs.

Field of Interest   Area of particular interest to the funder and the focus of program service within an agency. There are many different groups and sub-groups but common ones are the arts, environment, education, youth, education, health, religion, and women's services. The purpose of a grant writer is to carefully match the passions and objectives within the funder's field of interest with the actual and proposed programs of the agency seeking funds.

Final Report   Written report required by most funders at the end of the grant period that describes program results and how the funds were spent.

Financial Report   Accounting statement detailing income from all sources, expenses, assets, and liabilities. Most foundations require the previous year's financial report as an attachment to the proposal. Many require that it be audited by an outside firm and some ask for an itemized account of how grant funds were spent.

Fiscal Sponsorship   Formal relationship between a nonprofit organization and an individual or unincorporated organization that allows the person or organization without tax exempt status to have access to contributions from foundations, individuals, corporations, and government agencies.

Fiscal Year   Most of us operate on a calendar year from January 1 to December 31. Many nonprofits and school districts follow a different financial (fiscal) year that begins July 1 and ends June 30. The federal government's fiscal year is now October 1 to September 30. It's important to know and mesh the funder's fiscal year with the agency's calendar.

Formula Grants   Grants awarded by federal agencies on the basis of a set formula such as so many dollars per population, per capita income, or enrollment. Chief recipients are state governments who in turn make grants for education, substance abuse, mental health, and criminal justice programs.

Foundation   The word "foundation" has no legal meaning in and of itself. In common usage, however, it means a nongovernmental, nonprofit organization that serves the public good primarily through the making of grants to other nonprofit organizations.

FTE   Full-Time Equivalent. Because not all people paid under a grant will be working full time or have 100 percent of their salaries covered by the grant, budget forms ask for FTEs or the percentage of time staff spend for each position. An FTE can range from miniscule for an executive director or senior research scientist in an advisory capacity (0.05 FTE or 5 percent, which is 4 hrs/wk.) to more than one for multiple people with the same job title (4.2 FTE for 7 child care workers each working 30 hrs/wk).

Funding Cycle   A chronological pattern of proposal review, decision making, and applicant notification.

Giving Circle   New trend based on old traditions of philanthropy where individual members, local business firms, and community organizations pool their funds and other resources to address needs of a specific area or population— sometimes called social investment clubs.

Goals   The vision or end results of your project. Goals are more general and lofty than objectives but don't make them impossible to reach.

Grantee   The individual or organization that receives a grant.

Grant Monitoring   Ongoing assessment of the activities funded by the donor. This varies greatly among funding sources and can range from a yearly written report to monthly statistical program and financial accounting to onsite visits. It's important to know—and include—appropriate provisions for grant monitoring in the narrative section of the proposal.

Grantor   The individual or organization that makes the grant, also called funding sources or funders. While you are applying for a grant from a specific foundation or government department, you'll use their name or acronym to refer to the grantor. ("The NIH didn't come through so we're looking at Parsons.")

IHE   Institution of Higher Education, such as technical institutes, two-year community colleges, four-year colleges or universities.

In-Kind Contributions   Donated goods or services be raised. Some funders require the a percentage of the project budget through fundraising efforts and cash and in-kind donations.

IRS   The federal Internal Revenue Service, which grants agencies their tax-exempt status at approximately the same time the state attorney general's office is incorporating them as a nonprofit charitable corporation.

IRS Form 990   Information all public charities except religious groups and those whose gross incomes fall below $25,000 must file annually with the IRS.

IRS Form 990-PF   Same information required of private foundations in IRS Form 990. This is an important grant-writing tool since it provides financial information, names of directors or trustees, grant recipients, and amounts contributed during the year. Copies can be viewed online at www.GuideStar.org.

Joint Funding   A project supported by more than one grant maker.

LEA   Local Education Agency. This is usually a school district or the city/county agency charged with governing K–12 education. In some states, independent charter schools can serve as LEAs so read the fine print. (SEA is the state equivalent.)

Letter of Denial   A letter declining or rejecting your proposal. Some letters explain why the grant was not awarded, but most do not.

Letter of Intent (LOI)   A brief, often one-page, letter summarizing the grant request that is increasingly requested as a preliminary screening step by foundations. Since it's often difficult to write a summary before writing the entire proposal, an LOI requires all the planning decisions regarding a project are in place before you send it.

Leverage   Using a small amount of resources to gain a larger sum. Some funders specifically give a small amount of money with the express purpose of attracting different funds from other sources. An agency can also use its specialized knowledge, contacts in the community, facility, or other noncash resources as a lever to obtain funds and/or services from outside sources.

Limited-Purpose Foundation   A type of foundation that restricts its giving to one or very few fields of interest such as higher education or health. Often specific colleges, universities, hospitals, or research centers are named in the proposal guidelines, and proposals from other grant seekers are not accepted.

Logic Model   A process that visually depicts assumptions and elements of a specific program. They can be as simple as describing the situation, inputs, outputs, and outcomes in chart form or as elaborate as a circular flow chart with goals, resources, activities, outputs, and outcomes.

Matching Grant   A grant made with the specification that the amount donated must be matched with other funds according to a predetermined formula, sometimes one-to-one.

Mind Mapping   A form of brainstorming where words, ideas, and tasks are organized intuitively around a key word or idea with the goal of arranging components of a project in a graphic, nonlinear manner to disrupt the usual conceptual framework.

MOU   Memorandum of Understanding. Legal document spelling out what the lead agency/principal investigator and each collaborating group or individual will and will not do to implement the proposal. If funds and/or research and evaluation data are to be shared, these arrangements will need to be covered in great detail.

MSA   Metropolitan and Micropolitan Statistical Areas. Geographic areas used by the Census Bureau that have a high degree of social and economic integration. "Metro" areas have at least one urbanized core of 50,000 or more people and "micro" areas have one cluster of at least 10,000 residents.

NTEE   National Taxonomy of Exempt Entities. A comprehensive coding scheme developed by the National Center for Charitable Statistics for classifying nonprofit activities.

NPO   Nonprofit Organization. Technically applies to hospitals, colleges and universities, trade associations, chambers of commerce, civic groups, homeowners associations, and other groups with nonprofit status but in the grantsmanship arena it almost exclusively refers to groups that have 501(c)(3) standing.

Objectives   Specific measures of project goals. Objectives are the tangible expression of program ideas and concepts derived from the statement of need and supported by the work plan and budget.

Operating Expenses   Funds spent to keep the organization running on a day-to-day basis such as programs, salaries, facilities, utilities, office supplies, fundraising, insurance, and general administration. Until recently most foundations made a distinction between operating and program expenses and would not fund operating costs. This began to change in 2009 in response to the economic situation and more funds are now available for operating expenses. Guidelines for grants from the federal government specify the percentage allowed for administrative and/or overhead costs.

Operating Foundation   Private foundations that use the bulk of their income to run charitable programs of their own. They make few, if any, grants to outside groups.

Outcomes and Outputs   The results or consequences of program activities. Outcomes show the effects of the program (improved reading scores or staying clean and sober) as compared to outputs, which are more immediate program elements (number of workshops held or number of research subjects). Outcomes tend to be qualitative and outputs tend to be quantitative.

Pass–Through Grant   Money from one source that goes to another entity to distribute. Usually the funds come from the federal government and pass through the relevant state office to pay for programs administered by cities, agencies, or research institutes. Technically, when an agency serving as a fiscal agent for a smaller organization receives an award, it retains legal responsibility and the money is not considered a pass-through grant.

Performance Indicators   Data-based measurements that indicate progress toward achieving outcomes.

Pilot Project   Projects undertaken as a test to see if an approach or strategy works in addressing a specific problem.

Philanthropy   The overall term that covers voluntary giving by an individual or group to promote the common good and improve the quality of life— "giving and sharing beyond the family."

Planning Grant   This type of grant supports work on developing a change in direction or the establishment of a major new program emphasis and enables you to research community needs, visit programs similar to one you're considering, consult with experts, involve constituents in the program design, and do other planning activities to move a nebulous idea to an organized project ready for implementation.

Private Foundation   Established and supported primarily by private funds to conduct its own programs or to make donor-advised grants to other nonprofit organizations.

Private Support   Money received from individuals, foundations, corporations, clubs, and associations.

Program Officer   A staff member of a government agency, foundation, or corporate giving program who administers the application process. This is usually the person who has practical answers to questions about a funding opportunity you are researching.

Public Foundation A foundation that receives at least one-third of its income from the general public. It may provide direct charitable services as well as make grants.

Public Support Money received from the government.

Qualitative Research Research that deals with descriptions and involves analysis of data such as words (e.g., interviews), pictures (e.g., video), or objects (e.g., an artifact). The researcher is the data gathering instrument—interpretation of events is important.

Quantitative Research Research that deals with numbers and focuses on analysis of data that can be measured. Researcher uses tools such as questionnaires or equipment to collect numerical data—seeks precise measurement and analysis of target concepts.

Questorming A variant of brainstorming where the emphasis is on creating well-stated and well-selected questions or problem formulations rather than solving a problem or generating new ideas.

Research Funding Grants made for a well-defined test of a theory or to conduct research most often awarded to a specific person in an academic or research institution.

Restricted Funds All grant funds are restricted to the use specified in the funding application and subsequent contract.

RFP Request for Proposal. Formal printed announcement of available funds with guidelines on how to apply for them. Also known as an RFA (Request for Funding Assistance), NOFA (Notice of Funding Availability), SGA (Solicitation for Grant Applications), FFO (Federal Funding Opportunity), FOA (Funding Opportunity Announcement), and probably a dozen more before the second printing of this book.

ROI Return on Investment. A business tool used to measure the efficiency and effectiveness of an investment that is increasingly being used in the nonprofit world. While they are not interchangeable, the cost-benefit analysis and ROI are often linked.

The ROI can be found by using the following formula:

$$ROI = \frac{(\text{Gain from Investment} - \text{Cost of Investment})}{\text{Cost of Investment}}$$

Seed Money Funds given to a small project in the early stage of its development to nurture it through the formative stages. Often used interchangeably with a "pilot project," but seed funding usually is for an earlier stage that requires additional planning and development to test its feasibility and effectiveness.

Self-sufficiency   The extent to which a nonprofit is able to continue operating without relying on foundation grants or public sector subsidies. Can also be used to describe a goal for clients to live independent lives without support from the agency.

SF-424   Standard Form 424. This is the basic cover form for most federal grant applications. Even though it's supposed to be a "standard form," several agencies use variants and the online version you find in Grants.gov application files is different from the paper versions—so SF-424s are not "standard" and you need to read the fine print.

Site Visit   A visit to the grantee's office and/or program site by representatives of a funding source that is often combined with meeting staff, board, and service recipients.

SSPOC   Single-State Point of Contact. A state contact an organization must use when applying for many federal grants.

STEM   Science, Technology, Engineering and Math. A shortcut commonly used in NSF and Department of Education proposals.

Statistical Significance   A result can be called statistically significant if it is unlikely to have occurred by chance.

Stimulus Package   Officially called the "American Recovery and Reinvestment Act of 2009," this federal legislation authorized billions of dollars in program funding and tax cuts.

Sustainability   The expectation that ongoing funds to continue the research or project will be raised from other sources when the grant expires. Both government and foundation applications often ask for a sustainability plan.

TANF   Temporary Assistance for Needy Families. A federal grant program to implement major elements of welfare reform legislation. Because TANF programs vary from state to state, you need to be extremely well-versed in focus and requirements in your area if you propose services to people receiving this assistance.

Technical Assistance   Management or operational assistance given in such areas as fundraising, budgeting, program planning, legal advice, marketing, etc.

TIN   Taxpayer Identification Number. A nine-digit alternative to an EIN (Employer Identification Number) that is used by individuals for registering for government grants.

Uncompensated Care   Services, usually physical or mental health care, delivered free of charge to the user.

Unrelated Business Income   Income earned from the sale of products or services that are not directly related to the charitable purpose of a nonprofit organization.

Unrestricted Funds   Money not specifically designated to particular uses by the donor. Most often found in community foundations for funds where restrictions have expired or been removed.

Venture Philanthropy   Principles traditionally associated with venture capitalists to improve the capacity or performance of a nonprofit through a combination of funding and expertise that typically involves a more direct, sustained relationship, long-term funding, performance monitoring, and an exit strategy.

Virtual Foundation   Refers to the transition from grant making through mail and face-to-face meetings to grant making by email and Internet transfers.

Wet Signature   A signature on paper rather than a faxed or emailed copy. Some RFPs require the signature to be in blue ink for authenticity because blue doesn't copy.

Work Plan   An outline, graph, chart, or narrative that describes the steps to be taken to achieve the desired results. Sometimes called a "methods plan."

Resources

About.com http://nonprofit.about.com—Blog that covers a wild range of topics of interest to nonprofit professionals including grant writing, marketing, trends in philanthropy, other blogs of note, fundraising, agency profiles, and program ideas.

Adopt a Classroom www.adoptaclassroom.org—Donors choose a registered classroom and make an online donation so that teachers can get credit from affiliated vendors for out-of-pocket classroom supplies.

American Community Survey www.census.gov.acs.—Yearly survey conducted by the U.S. Census Bureau to update general demographic information between mandated decennial surveys.

American FactFinder http://factfinder.census.gov—Source of all census data including specialized updates in key areas—easy-to-access information to zip code level with much information available by census track in advanced searches.

American Grant Writer's Association (AGWA) www.agws.us—For-profit training and networking group that offers an in-house Certified Grant Writer Credential—different from the Grant Professionals Association, which also offers validated, accredited credentialing and educational opportunities for people interested in the grants community. (See listing under GPA).

Black Gives Back www.BlackGivesBack.com—Blog that tracks African-American philanthropy.

Blue Avocado www.blueavocado.org—"practical, provocative, and fun food-for-thought for nonprofit board members"—excellent source for educating a board about how grants fit into a larger picture.

California Health Interview Survey   www.chis.org—While the specific data applies only to California residents, the questionnaire topics and the detailed picture of the health and health-care needs of California's large and diverse population are excellent examples of information that is important in establishing the community's need for proposed projects.

Council for Advancement and Support of Education (CASE)   www.case.org— Higher education's leading resource for knowledge, standards, advocacy and training in alumni relations, communications, fundraising, marketing, and related activities—local chapters sometimes allow nonacademic visitors to monthly meetings.

Charity Channel   www.charitychannel.com—Articles and book reviews about nonprofit management including grant writing—summaries are free; yearly "membership" is $37.

Charity How To   www.charityhowto.com—Free and moderately priced marketing and fundraising tutorials for nonprofits who want to learn to use Facebook, Twitter, and other social networking tools.

Chronicle of Philanthropy   www.philanthropy.com—Digest of news articles, conference reports, blogs, books, etc., in the philanthropic arena.

Dial 2-1-1   www.211.org—National site to locate regional contacts for comprehensive human and social service information and referral services that can provide current, local data regarding community needs.

Donors Choose   www.donorschoose.org—Online funding source for school materials requested by classroom and frontline school personnel in the $100 to $400 range plus a listing of other funding sources for classroom teachers.

Fiscal Sponsor Directory   www.fiscalsponsordirectory.org—National directory with informative articles on how to locate and work with a fiscal sponsor if you do not have tax exemption as a 501(c)(3) organization.

(The) Foundation Center   www.fiscalsponsordirectory.org—Comprehensive listing of public and private grant-making foundations, community foundations, and corporate giving programs—regional libraries, research reports, newsletters, blogs, webinars, anything and everything you want to know about grantsmanship—their *Proposal Writing Short Course* is a succinct review of both the why's and how-to's of preparing a proposal from start to finish. (http://foundationcenter.org/getstarted/tutorials/shortcourse/)

(The) Free Management Library   http://managementhelp.org/eval/fnl_eval .htm—An integrated online library of management how-to's for nonprofits and for-profits with free downloadable articles.

Funds for Writers   www.fundsforwriters.com.—Both free and subscription newsletters listing grants, competitions, and other money-making contacts for individual writers.

GrantGopher   http//www.grantgopher.com—Subscription source of foundation and grant information, free weekly bulletin.

Grants.gov   www.grants.gov—The portal to find ALL federal grants and funding agencies—access to complete RFPs, funding legislation, federal departments and agencies—site of online application process for most, but not all, federal grants—free registration to receive notification of new grant opportunity postings.

(The) Grant Goddess   http://grantgoddess.blogspot.com—Delightful blog sharing the joys and frustrations of writing grants from Veronica Robbins and her associates at Creative Resources and Research. The firm is also one of many places you can outsource your grant writing and program evaluation. (www.grantgoddess.com)

GrantsNet   www.grantsnet.org—Online searchable grants database sponsored by the American Association for the Advancement of Science that focuses on biomedical and science education, research, and funding.

(The) Grantsmanship Center   The premier grants training institution in the United States whose "Program Planning and Proposal Writing" is the most widely read publication in nonprofit history. Offers 150 grantsmanship workshops annually. Free resources include weekly email newsletter, announcements from the *Federal Register*, indexes of funding sources, and archives of articles from their monthly magazine.

Grant Professionals Association (GPA)   www.grantprofessional.org—Membership organization that encourages the professionalism of the field through conferences, publications, and local chapters. Developed the Grant Professional Certification Institute's (http://grantscredential.org) certification program that is the first accredited, validated certification for grant professionals. Formerly known as the American Association of Grant Professionals and sometimes confused with the American Grant Writer's Association.

Grant Station   www.grantstation.com—An interactive online grants database web site that connects grant seekers with information about grant makers that are actively accepting inquiries and proposals—expensive for a beginner to join ($699/year) but articles and limited information about funders are free.

Grant Writing Newsletter www.grantwritingnewsletter.com—Free newsletter with basic how-to's published by consultant Phil Johncock who also provides online grantsmanship training.

Grassroots Institute for Fundraising Training (GIFT) www.grassrootsfundraising .org—Combination of online and onsite, free and fee-based technical assistance in nonprofit management and funding diversity for small organizations, particularly those working on social justice issues.

Great Lakes Directory www.greatlakesdirectory.org—Database of foundations in the Great Lakes area that fund environmental issues.

Guide Star www.guidestar.org—Comprehensive listing and comparisons of all charitable organizations that file an IRS 990 form—used by many foundations to verify status of agencies requesting funds—allows agencies to build a profile of themselves.

Independent Sector www.independentsector.org—A coalition of corporations, foundations, and private voluntary organizations that works to strengthen America's nonprofit organizations—publications and research with a focus on public policy.

Institute of Museum and Library Services www.imls.gov—Primary source of federal support for the nation's 123,000 libraries and 17,500 museums. Good program ideas and sample proposals. Easy to navigate site with funding alerts and online application process.

IssueLab www.issuelab.org—Compilation of research about social issues gleaned from nonprofit, foundation, and academic sources that is searchable by issue and geography. Free registration for daily research updates and monthly e-newsletter.

W. K. Kellogg Foundation www.wkkf.org—Research reports on trends and issues in philanthropy plus grants supporting children, families, racial equity, and civic engagement. A comprehensive free Logic Model Development Guide is available from www.wkkf.org/knowledge-center/resources/2010/ Logic-Model-Development-Guide.aspx.

Kickstarter www.kickstarter.com—Online opportunity to solicit funds for individual projects directly by describing proposed activities, setting a financial goal and campaign time frame, and providing incentives for pledges.

Mira's List http://miraslist.blogspot.com—Foundations, residencies, fellowships, deadlines, interviews, and other resources for artists, writers, composers, and others in the fine arts.

National Association for the Exchange of Industrial Resources (NAEIR) www.naeir.org—Nonprofit gifts-in-kind organization that facilitates the exchange of excess inventory between companies from across the United States and deserving schools, churches, and nonprofit organizations.

National Assembly of State Arts Agencies (NASAA) www.sasaa-arts.org— State by state listing of arts councils and agencies with address, contacts, and links to state web site and email.

Open Directory www.dmoz.org—limited database of funding sources for some categories not usually listed like sports, gender, sexual preference, ethnic, and multiracial projects.

Pamela's Grantwriting Blog www.pamelasgrantwritingblog.com—Practical systems and relevant information for one-person development offices and grassroots organizations that includes individual giving, grants development, web and social media strategies, donor communication, and public relations tactics.

Philanthropy News Digest www.foundationcenter.org—This is one of two regular online publications the Foundation Center produces to help you stay abreast of trends in giving patterns, major grant awards, personnel and funding changes in foundations, and other news in the philanthropic arena. The other is the *RFP Bulletin* which lists funding opportunities on a weekly basis.

Principal Investigators Association www.principalinvestigators.org— Professional membership organization for lead scientists in all forms of research that publishes free weekly eAlerts available to nonmembers interested in both the science and nonscience responsibilities of managing a grant; especially good coverage of ethical and collaborative issues.

Publication Coach www.publicationcoach.com—Daphne Gray-Grant is a writing and editing coach who offers a free, very brief, weekly newsletter and occasional articles that are fun to read and useful for anyone who writes for other people.

The School Funding Center www.schoolfundingcenter.info—Monitors more than 4,000 web sites, newsletters, and other grant sources in one central database where educators can find every federal, state, and foundation grant available to their schools.

(My) School Grantsm www.discountschoolsupply.com—A free grant database designed to help teachers find the funds needed for the classroom—articles to help with writing and winning a grant.

7-11

Seliger & Associates   www.seliger.com—Grant writing, grant source research, and related services for public and nonprofit agencies, as well as selected businesses and individuals—free blog that translates and debunks bureaucratic language and pretensions.

SOFII   Showcase of Fundraising Innovation and Inspiration www.sofii.org—Free comprehensive, easily accessible archive of creative fundraising ideas from around the world.

United Way of America   One of its services is the Outcome Measurement Resource Network (www.liveunited.org/outcomes), which offers a series of free articles on outcome measurement including logic models and performance measurement in government settings. Local United Way chapters are often excellent sources of current, relevant information on community needs and resources.

Western Carolina University   www.wcu.edu—Publishes excellent listing of directories, handbooks, and manuals, and web sites for people seeking research grants.

Writing It Real   www.writingitreal.com.—Sheila Bender's subscription newsletter and editing service for poets and personal essayists that is useful in honing your writing and editing skills.

Yahoo! Real Estate Neighborhood Profiles   http://realestate.yahoo.com/neighborhoods—A good starting place for basic demographics on population, housing, schools, employment, etc., for a city or zip code.